A Year Off... A Year On?

About the author

Since graduating with a degree in English from Leeds University and successfully completing a Diploma in Careers Guidance, Suzanne Straw has worked in a variety of positions within the Careers Service. She has worked with young people in schools, colleges and on government training schemes and with the unemployed and adults. In addition to careers work, she has taught English GCSE and BTEC Core Skills in evening classes.

Suzanne currently works for London Central Careers Unit as a specialist careers adviser covering legal, secretarial and public sector careers and opportunities in continental Europe. In addition, she is a UK Euro-adviser for EURES (European Employment Services).

Throughout her career, Suzanne has written articles for a variety of careers and educational journals, including COIC. Since joining London Central Careers Unit in 1992, she has written a number of publications covering the legal professions, work and study opportunities in Europe, secretarial work, the Civil Service, paramedical careers and how to write a convincing CV.

Suzanne enjoys reading the classics, going to the cinema and theatre and sport. She particularly enjoys cycling, tennis and squash. She is also a keen traveller. Over the past ten years, she has backpacked around Europe, Asia, South Africa, Australia and New Zealand. Next stop, South America.

A Year Off... A Year On?

A guide to jobs, voluntary service, conservation project and working holidays in the UK and overseas during your education

Suzanne Straw

Student Helpbook Series

HOBSONS

CRAC

ISBN 1 86017 016 1

A CIP catalogue record for this book is available from the British Library.

CRAC

The Careers Research and Advisory Centre (CRAC) is a registered educational charity. Hobsons Publishing PLC produces CRAC publications under exclusive licence and royalty agreements.

Printed and bound in Great Britain by Clays Ltd, St Ives plc, Bungay, Suffolk.
Text design by Leah Klein

Ref L251/B/8/qq/E/JF

HOBSONS

Contents

1 Introduction

2 Taking Time Out in the UK

3 Taking Time Out in Continental Europe

4 Taking Time Out Worldwide

5 Appendices

1

Introduction

About this Book

This book looks at a variety of opportunities that are available to young people and adults who want to take time out after school or college, before going on to employment or university, after university or at any time in their lives.

Time out, if spent constructively, can provide you with many benefits. You are likely to gain life skills such as independence, confidence and maturity as well as make new friends, broaden your horizons and have a good time.

Employers recruiting graduates, who are faced with hundreds of application forms, look for something 'extra' in candidates to be selected for interview. People who have taken time out and done something useful, exciting, adventurous and/or relevant to the job they are applying for, usually catch employers' eyes. Employers' views of graduates who have taken time out are covered in more detail in chapter 5.

University admissions tutors, also, are generally very positive about students who are planning to take a year out before university or college of higher education. Like employers, most admissions tutors are impressed by the experience and maturity which a job, study abroad, travel or voluntary service can bring. Admissions tutors' views are covered in more detail in chapter 6.

In this book, you will also find more than 16 case-studies of people who have taken time out to pursue a variety of activities. When interviewing them, they all impressed me with their great enthusiasm and each of them recommended that other people should follow in their footsteps.

There are many organisations mentioned in this book that give their workers or employees a lot of support to help them fit into their new environment. Going abroad, for example, is not so scary when you have an organisation to contact if things aren't going to plan. There is also much scope to be adventurous and to 'go it alone' but be careful and plan well. Get advice from people who have been involved in similar activities in the past. See chapters 15 and 20 for help and advice on planning a safe and exciting trip.

A year out, or time out, is not just an option for school/college students, prior to employment or higher education, or for graduates before permanent employment. It is an option for anyone at any time in their life and career. It is also an option for the confident 16 year old who wants to take some time out after GCSEs/NVQs/Standard Grades or equivalent before further study or employment. Time out can often change the direction of your life.

In this book, you will find details of vacation, short-term and longer-term opportunities for work, study and voluntary service in the UK, continental Europe and all over the world. You will also find information on exchanges and travel. Some organisations are geared up to providing opportunities for a specific age group. Some will cater for the 16–18 year old still in education, others cater for those wanting to take a gap year, for graduates, and for people of any age or background. Because of the growing importance of the European Union, and Britain's place within it, a lot of emphasis has been given to opportunities in Europe where you can improve your language skills and prepare for a long-term career with a European dimension. At whatever stage it's taken, time out should be seen as part of your development and education of life. What you gain in your time out will, in most cases, be useful in your long-term career and you can plan your experiences to help you achieve your career goals.

Don't just think about taking time out, go ahead! If you plan your time well you should gain great rewards. And… it may change your life!

Suzanne Straw

1 Time Out Options

If you are thinking about taking some time out, there is a variety of options available to you. Take note of the points made in the following chapters and think carefully about what you want to achieve in your time out. When you return to study, or full-time employment, you will have to justify your decision and explain what you have gained as a person.

Firstly, you need to decide if you want to spend your time out in the UK, in continental Europe or further afield. You may decide to spend some time in the UK first saving money and then spend the rest of your time abroad.

The main options

In the UK, continental Europe and in other parts of the world, the main options open to you are:

- work – paid or voluntary
- study – formal or informal
- travel – organised or independent.

WORK

Work can be divided into paid or voluntary. Some paid work will not pay much, some voluntary work pays a small allowance. The main difference between these types of work is that in paid work you will be part of a commercial, money-making operation and in voluntary work you will be part of an organisation that serves the wider community.

Paid work

This can be short-term, for example during the summer, or long-term, for up to a year or more. There are many opportunities, particularly for short-term work. You could, for example, work on a campsite in the UK, as a sales representative in Italy, in a hotel in France, on a ski resort in Switzerland, as an au pair in the Canary Islands, as a teacher in Japan or as a children's camp counsellor in America.

If you decide to work in your time out, your main priority may be to take the best-paid job which will enable you to finance a trip abroad, or, if you are going to university or college, to save money to support yourself during your studies. Alternatively, you may decide that your priority is to gain some work experience related to a profession you are keen to enter. For some professions, for example social work, nursing, paramedical careers and conservation work, relevant experience is an advantage, sometimes even a requirement, when applying for professional courses. Course or career-related employment will be the most useful work experience you can gain.

Voluntary work

If you decide to undertake voluntary work, you will find that there is a wide variety of possibilities in the UK and abroad. You will need to decide what type of voluntary work interests you. You will be able to choose between working in the community among people in need such as children, the elderly, the disabled, the poor, the homeless, or working on the land, or with animals or on environmental or conservation projects.

STUDY

Study can be divided into formal study – at school or college – and informal study – learning about a country's language and culture by living there, usually with a family.

Formal study

You may want to spend some of your time out studying. In the UK, you could learn some keyboard and computing skills to help you in your future studies or career, take a course in teaching English as a foreign language (TEFL) or enrol on a foreign language course. In continental Europe and in countries worldwide, you could attend language and summer schools or spend a full academic year at a school or university. There are also a number of European Union exchange programmes which enable students to spend some time studying in another European country, while studying for a UK degree or HND. If you prefer something more physical, you might want to learn to teach skiing or to gain a sports instructor qualification.

Informal study

There are opportunities worldwide for people to stay with families as paying guests with the aim of learning the language and about the country's culture. There are also several organisations which arrange for young people to go on exchange visits abroad and live with families while attending school there.

TRAVEL

Again, there are many ways to travel and see something of the world but essentially you can either travel with an organised group or independently.

Organised travel

If you can raise the finances and sponsorship, you may want to consider spending a few months in one of the developing regions of the world. You could travel with a group and get involved in a social or environmental project. You might live in close quarters with other people and, no doubt, you would learn a great deal about yourself. Joining this kind of project enables you to combine voluntary work with seeing new areas of the world. It's a safe way of travelling, especially if you are young and/or inexperienced.

You could also think about going on an adventurous holiday to areas such as Asia, Africa and South America. There are many organisations which specialise in small group exploratory holidays.

If you want to travel abroad and pick up short-term work, there are organisations that will help you by arranging visas and work permits.

Independent travel

You may decide to go it alone and to organise your travels independently. If this is what you want, you will need to plan well ahead and have enough money to finance your travels. There are several travel agents that specialise in student travel, long-haul flights and around-the-world itineries.

In later chapters on opportunities available in the UK, other parts of Europe and the rest of the world, you will find much more detail on the variety of options available to you and details of organisations that you can contact. In the Reading List in Part 5, you will find details of other books to refer to and other sources of information.

2 When Should You Take Time Out?

Taking time out is becoming more and more popular and people are deciding to take a break from study or employment at different stages of their lives. Traditionally, it has been mainly young people who have taken a year out, or a 'gap' year, before, or after, higher education, but now the idea is becoming more popular with people who want to take a break during their career, or when changing career direction.

Some young people decide to take time out at 16 and there are some organisations that will arrange for them to spend time studying abroad before they return to continue their education in the UK. In this book, you will find details of some organisations that specialise in arranging activities for gap-year students. There are also many organisations that are flexible about the age range of people who participate in their programmes. In fact, some, such as Voluntary Service Overseas, favour older applicants who have gained experience of life and of particular professions. So it's never too late to satisfy those itchy feet and that desire for new adventures and experiences...

The easiest time to take a break, however, is at 16 or 18, before A-levels (or the equivalent) or higher education, or before starting work. Schools, colleges, universities and employers are used to this idea and many are in favour of it.

Deferred UCAS entry

If you intend to take time out before going on to higher education, you will need to consider when you will apply to university via UCAS (Universities and Colleges Admissions Service). It is possible to apply to university for deferred entry. Students apply to UCAS between

September and mid-December with the intention of starting their course the following September/October. Rather than starting your course the following year, you can opt to defer it to the next year and take a year out in between. Alternatively, you can apply to higher education institutions after you receive your A-level/BTEC National/Advanced GNVQ/Highers results. This means, though, that you will have to keep an eye on your applications during your year out. If you are applying for courses for which applicants are interviewed, you will have to be available to attend these from January to March of your year out.

It is more sensible to apply for deferred entry. You can then relax during your year out knowing that you have a place in higher education confirmed. You will also not have to spend any of your time out researching courses, filling in the UCAS form and attending interviews.

If you apply for deferred entry, you will need to explain what you intend to do in your year out on your UCAS form. Admissions tutors want to know that you have thought through what you want to do and achieve, and that you will be using your time constructively. It is, therefore, important that you plan your year out well ahead.

Justifying your decision

If you are considering taking a break at 16 or 18 before going on to employment, after graduation, or during your career, you will need to think carefully about how you will justify your decision and market the benefits of it on your return to the employment market-place. You need to make sure that you will be doing something constructive and worthwhile from which you will gain experience and new life skills. Generally, you will have gained so much as far as life and personal skills go that this should not be too difficult. It is important to be aware, though, that some employers can be traditional in their attitudes and sometimes view people who take time out as flighty and unable to stick at things. You know that this is not true but you will need to be aware of the assumptions that some employers may make and anticipate these when filling in application forms and answering questions at interviews.

However, time out is not for everyone. Depending on what you do, you may get out of a working routine, you may have to rough it or work in a close-knit community with people of differing ages and cultures. You may not have a regular income and the security of family and friends around you. You need to think carefully about the uncertainties that may face you and if you will rise to the challenge or if you will miss your security.

In this book you will find 16 case-studies of people who have taken time out at different stages of their life. You should find their stories encouraging and you will be able to read about what they have all gained from their varied experiences.

For many, the opportunity to take time out should not be missed. If you want to do it, whatever your age and stage in life, you should be able to find something challenging and worthwhile. If you want to do it, do. You do not want to regret wasted opportunities later on. And if you plan it well and have the right attitude, you could experience the best times of your life...

Tony McDonald

Time out after GCSEs case-study

Tony is now at Leeds Metropolitan University studying for a joint degree in politics and economics. He's 22 and he took four years off before going back to college to take his A-levels.

❛ I did quite well at school and left with eight good GCSEs not wanting to carry on studying. I felt I needed a break and I wanted to earn some money. So, for about a year, I did different practical jobs working as a welder and a car upholsterer but eventually decided that, at 17, I wanted more excitement in my life. I wanted to explore Europe and felt that Spain was a good place to start.

Some contacts of mine helped me to get a job in Barcelona with one of the construction companies that was building athletes' hotels for the Olympic Games. I worked as a labourer doing odd jobs like painting, humping bricks around and some basic bricklaying. The money was great – £80 a day – and I was able to save a lot of it because I lived in a caravan on site. I knew some Spanish, after studying it at GCSE, and I got to know some of the best bars and clubs in Barcelona!

This really gave me the taste for European travel and I went on to do bar work in Germany and Portugal and picked grapes in the Loire valley. Most of the time I stayed in youth hostels and got by with basic German and French. I did find it difficult communicating in Portugal, though. I got the grape-picking job through an ad in the *Daily Mail*. It was really hard work but the weather was brilliant.

I returned to the UK but couldn't shake off the travel bug. I wanted to see a bit of America and a friend in San Diego managed to arrange a job for me on a children's summer camp. I worked there for three months. The children were aged between 10 and 15 and part of my job was to teach them baseball. This was a bit of a problem at first as I hadn't played it before! However, I just thought "rounders with a big bat" and soon had it sussed. I got $4 an hour with free food and accommodation. The weather was superb and I liked the American kids; they were loud and bubbly. I made a lot of friends, most of whom were American college students.

By now, I'd saved quite a bit of money and was ready for some serious travelling; for the next six months I travelled all over the USA, from San Diego north as far as Seattle through Los Angeles, San Francisco and Portland. Then I went through the middle of the country to Kansas

City and Chicago and further south to Nashville and across to Dallas. Further west I went to Denver and New Mexico and on to Arizona to see the Grand Canyon. Coming back to San Diego I managed a stop at Las Vegas. I loved America and had what have been the best times of my life so far travelling around there. I mainly travelled by train and shared lifts. Nights were spent in hostels and backpackers at an average price of about $8–$15 a night.

Towards the end of the trip I made a decision that, when I got back to the UK, I was ready to return to study and wanted to go to university. This meant I had to spend the next two years taking A-levels which was difficult at first but then I began to reap the benefits of my travels. I felt I had matured and had a much more positive attitude to study – I definitely didn't have this at 16.

I would really recommend time out to people. In my case it was the right choice because I was unsettled and immature and couldn't put my mind to more studying. My time out made me more self-sufficient and worldly; I'm not scared of much now. Travel also makes you more broad-minded and tolerant and you don't get so uptight about life. However, I wouldn't advise people to take as many years out as I did. Four years away can make it hard for you to get back into study. I'm in my first year of university now and I've got three years of serious study ahead of me! ’

3 Planning Ahead and Finance

If you intend to take some time out, you should aim to start researching the possibilities open to you at least a year before you take time out. For some options, you will need to raise finance and you will need to apply early to most of the organisations offering opportunities. If you intend to apply to higher education, you will have to have some idea of what you plan to do a year before.

If you decide to work in the UK

It is unlikely that you will need to save money but you will need to start applying to organisations and contacting employers about six months before you hope to start work. You will need to compile a CV and find out what the employment situation is like in the area in which you intend to work. You may want to apply for jobs on holiday camps, as an au pair or teaching English as a foreign language and for jobs in these areas early application is essential. You may also need to gain some relevant experience before applying. If you plan to work in shops, hotels, restaurants or on building sites, you could try getting a part-time job and increase your hours into a full-time job later. If you intend to do temporary office work, you might need to do an intensive secretarial course before you sign on with agencies in order to increase your chances of employment.

If you plan to work abroad

You should research organisations that offer opportunities and apply early. If your plan is to go alone, find out about the employment, or unemployment, situation and which organisations you should contact when looking for work. In most European countries, you will need a reasonable understanding of the language for most jobs; for some, you will need good written and spoken language skills. Often, you will need to pay for your own air fare and insurance. Exceptions to this include au pair work, Camp America and Bunacamp where air fare and insurance are paid for you; these opportunities are popular so apply early.

If you intend to study abroad

There is some scope for scholarships but you need to research these thoroughly and apply early. Useful books to refer to are listed in Part 5 and should be available in university careers libraries and in large local libraries.

There are also many European Union-funded programmes, which will come under the umbrella of the new Socrates and Leonardo programmes. These fund students in higher education to spend time on study or work placement in other parts of Europe. These are mentioned in more detail in Part 3.

If you want to travel

You will need to save a fairly substantial amount of money; you may need to work in the UK for several months first. Those who decide to do work in the community, join workcamps or do conservation work will generally have to pay for fares and insurance and may have to pay an organisation a fee for sorting out a placement. Organisations that run expeditions or adventure holidays usually expect participants to raise £1,000–£3,000 via donations and sponsorship; if this option is your choice you'll need plenty of time to raise the cash.

You will find that, for most of the options you can choose, you will need money, so it's worth getting a part-time job during your school/college studies or, if you are established in a career, saving as much of your salary as you can. Most people who take time out do not have access to any sponsorship, scholarships or funds and rely entirely on their own finances. They use their own initiative, live sparingly and save as much as possible from temporary jobs. If they opt for voluntary work in their time out, they may have to raise money initially for flight, insurance and organisation fee, but when they are working they will often be given pocket money and board and lodging may be free.

So, get saving, get planning, get applying and the world's your oyster.

4 Advantages and Disadvantages of Taking Time Out

It is important to think through your decision to take time out carefully and to consider the pros and cons. Some advantages and disadvantages are listed below.

The advantages

- It gives you time to take a break from employment or study and consider your future. Many students who take time out and come back to the UK to study in higher education completely change their choice of course.
- You can travel the world, broaden your horizons, meet new people, experience different cultures and make new friends. You can learn about yourself and learn self-reliance.
- You can gain valuable work experience in jobs either related, or unrelated, to your choice of career. Most work experience will enable you to develop very valuable skills such as communication, working as a member of a team, negotiation, dealing with the public, numeracy, organisational... the list goes on. If you have decided upon your final career, relevant work experience gained in a year out can give you a head start when you are applying for jobs later.
- You are likely to become more mature, responsible, self-aware, flexible and independent, and more easily able to cope with new situations and challenges.
- What you have achieved and gained should make you attractive to employers and to higher education admissions tutors.
- If you take a break, and will be going back to study on your return, you will probably be ready to throw yourself into your academic work with enthusiasm.

- If you work in the UK for most of the year, you could save some money which will be useful, particularly if you will be going on to higher education.
- You are likely to have an excellent time; the majority of people who take time out and do something adventurous with it say that they have no regrets and that they had the best times of their lives.

The disadvantages

- You have to return to the routine of life again; you may find it hard to adjust to this lifestyle after your exciting and adventurous time out.
- If you want to go into employment after your time out, you will have to work hard tracking down vacancies and employers. You may want to give this some thought before you go away and think about the best time to apply for jobs. Returning from a year out in September, for example, to look for a job is not a good idea since most employers will have already filled their vacancies with recent school-leavers and graduates. It would be better to return in January or February and get a head start.
- If you will be going on to further study after your time out, you may take a little time to adjust to an academic life again. Science, maths and engineering students, in particular, often find that they have forgotten a lot in their time out and they have to work hard in the first few months to keep up with people who have gone to university straight after their A-levels.
- If you're not careful about your finances, you could end the time out with no money and perhaps in debt.

For advice on the pros and cons of taking a year out, speak to your local Careers Service.

Overall, there are many more advantages than disadvantages to taking time out. It is not a suitable option for everyone, though, and you need to make sure that you do not waste your time; time spent relaxing doing nothing will not impress anyone and you will gain very little. Those who do go for it should also be aware that, when they resume their studies or employment again, they may have some adjusting to do and may feel a bit disorientated to begin with.

And what about employers and higher education admissions tutors? What do they think about people who take time out? Read on for their views...

5 Employers' Views

When you decide to take some time out it is important to think long-term. Why do you want to take time out? What do you hope to gain? If possible, try to link your time out to your career goals by aiming to develop some relevant personal qualities and gain some related work experience.

When you are planning that year of your life, stop to think for a little while about what you want to do when you return to the job market and how you can prepare for this. How will you sell yourself and your experiences to employers?

If you intend to take time out after your degree, it would be sensible to apply for jobs in your final year so that you can gauge the competition and see what jobs are available and what employers are looking for. If you are offered a job, you could try to defer the start date for a year. If you are not successful in obtaining a job, then you will have gone through a useful process and, when you start looking for jobs again a year later, you will be well aware of what is expected of you.

In this chapter, you will find the views of some employers, recruiting for different industries, regarding students who take time out either before, or after, higher education. Most of the comments made will also be applicable to employers who recruit for non-graduate positions.

Coopers & Lybrand

Barbara Picheta, National Graduate Recruitment Manager

'When Coopers & Lybrand are recruiting trainee accountants we look favourably at people who have taken time out; the issue is what applicants have done

with their time. If applicants have gained useful experience and maturity then these are positive factors. Work experience in different contexts is particularly useful.

Recruiters ask about the time out in the interview and, if an applicant has travelled rather than worked, they look at what they have gained from this experience such as self-insight, self-reliance, a broad outlook on life and so on. Someone who has taken several years out, and started a variety of jobs or activities, and given them up, would have to convince Coopers & Lybrand that they will be able to stick to a career in accountancy.

Once they are satisfied that an applicant has gained useful work experience, and/or developed personal qualities in their time out, the recruiters look at the applicant's knowledge of accountancy as a profession. What research have they done into the career? Is it a rational career decision?

Coopers & Lybrand are now receiving an increasing number of applications from people who have taken time out, and an increasing number of applications from mature and overseas students, so people who have taken time out do not stand out from the crowd as much as they did in the past.'

Mercury Asset Management

Andrew Mair, Director

'Mercury Asset Management recruits graduates as trainee fund managers and trainee administrators.

Quite often, we find that applicants who have taken time out are more mature, clearer in their own minds, more self-aware and broad-minded and are better communicators than other applicants. They usually have additional qualities to offer as well as their intellectual capabilities. They tend to do better in the selection process since they have more to talk about and have more experiences to draw upon.

We look favourably upon people who have taken time out to see the world, and work experience gained during the year is very helpful. Those who have gained work experience know what the world of work is like and have a knowledge base against which they can judge Mercury Asset Management as an employer. Any work experience gained is helpful but work experience gained in financial services is ideal. Those who have gained financial work experience know what type of job they are applying for and are seen to have shown initiative. Mercury Asset Management offers summer work experience to a number of undergraduates.

Graduates who take time out before higher education are usually at an advantage in the selection process. However, graduates who take time out after university have to work harder for their application to catch the selector's eye. They are marginally disadvantaged as selectors tend to focus on the current crop of graduates. These applicants need to do a little more selling of the advantages they have gained in their time out and spend a bit more time justifying their decision. They need to be more creative in packaging themselves and approaching the market-place. A little more effort is required, that's all.

Applicants should think carefully about how they sell their experiences on the application form and should draw out the personal qualities that they have developed. Words such as communication skills, organisation, planning, enterprise and resilience can impress. A good idea is to send a letter in addition to the application form, and to use the letter to sell yourself. Interviewers explore the time out experiences in the interview. Time out can be character building. Those who don't take time out can sometimes come across as less worldly and less self-aware.

Generally, Mercury Asset Management's advice is, if you need to get travelling out of your system, or to take some time out, go ahead and do it while you're young. If you're not sure, do it anyway. However, do plan your time out carefully and spare a thought for what you will do when you return. Ideally, spend some of your time out undertaking some relevant work experience.'

Marks & Spencer

Hilary Woodland, Graduate Recruitment Manager

'Marks & Spencer takes on approximately 200 graduates, 25 A-level trainees and 25 job changers each year. Usually, about 18,000 people apply for these positions. Marks & Spencer likes graduates to apply in their final year of study and will sometimes defer successful candidates' entry dates.

When recruiting to any level, Marks & Spencer places much emphasis on managerial and personal skills which applicants have usually gained outside their studies. As long as applicants have used their time out constructively, the interview panel is impressed. In the initial interview they are looking for five key qualities:

- *leadership*
- *planning and organisation skills*
- *analytical ability*
- *assertiveness*
- *job motivation.*

All of these qualities could be developed during an applicant's time out.

Marks & Spencer looks at what applicants have done in the past and feels that past experiences are a predictor of future behaviour. Work experience gained and travel undertaken in time out can give applicants examples to draw upon in the interview and can help them demonstrate that they have the skills that are looked for. However, these skills can also be developed through individuals' involvement in clubs and societies and via summer employment. Marks & Spencer also likes to see that applicants have had some previous retail experience and that they have thought about retail as a career for several years – not just after their time out.

A year out can be valuable in that it can often give people more confidence and help them develop their personal qualities but it is definitely not essential to get them through the selection procedure.'

London Electricity

Judith Powell, Senior Development Adviser

'London Electricity recruits graduates for a range of trainee positions. The vast majority of our applicants have experience other than university life to draw upon such as vacation work, industrial placements or a year out.

When interviewing people who have taken time out, we look at what they have gained. We search for evidence of when applicants have, for example, coped with challenges, raised finance, used their initiative and gained experience of planning and organisation. We see it as an added bonus if someone has gained maturity and relevant work experience in their time out.

For our management positions, we look for people who have developed skills in leadership, planning, organisation, communication and team work. People who have taken time out are often able to draw on their experiences to demonstrate that they have these skills. Applicants have to justify what they did and why. London Electricity expects people to maximise the opportunities open to them. The graduate who has simply studied and passed a degree, and done nothing else, is rare in our application process and it is very unlikely that a candidate such as this would get to the interview stage.'

Logica

Judith Adamson, Graduate Recruitment Officer

'Logica is a software company that recruits approximately 170–200 graduates into systems analysis and systems support vacancies each year. We are a young company and look for people who are "all rounders". We like people who are flexible, good communicators and good team workers.

We look favourably upon people who have taken time out if the time has added to them as a person. We usually find that applicants who have taken time out are more mature, more independent, better communicators and more rounded people. Those who have used their time out constructively, and have written it up well on the application form, are more likely to get an interview. Useful experiences include voluntary work, adventurous travel and relevant (ie career-related) work experience.

Those who take time out after university must do this for the right reasons and package it well. If applicants can show that they thought carefully about why they wanted to take a break, and can discuss what they gained from it, the time out can only be advantageous. However, a year out may not be suitable for everyone.

The selectors usually find that graduates undersell themselves on the application form; those who have taken time out need to capitalise on what they have achieved and gained from it. In the interview, applicants need to show Logica that they are committed to the company and to the profession they are applying for. They need to make sure that their year out is not presented in a way so that it looks as though they have simply put off going into employment. Logica needs to

be convinced of an applicant's reliability and keen interest in the area of work they are applying for.

Logica's work is contract-based so sometimes we may be able to offer someone a job and let them defer their start date so that they can take some time out. However, we can not usually hold jobs open for a year; anyone who has been offered a job, but then wants to take some time out, would be advised to reapply.'

General points

Generally, employers look favourably upon people who have taken time out. However, it is important that, when applying for jobs, you *sell* what you have gained from your time out. Employers are usually looking for initiative, flexibility, good communication skills, the ability to work well in a team, organisational skills and, ideally, some relevant work experience. You need to match the experience and skills you have gained to the experience and skills the employer is looking for; in the majority of cases you should not find this difficult. If, during your time out, you have gained personal skills and a knowledge of work then you will be able to draw on your experiences and give many relevant examples in the interview. You are, in this way, likely to stand out from other applicants. For some professions, such as social work, a year's experience in a relevant environment is an entry requirement for the professional course.

People who take time out after their degree, rather than before, will have to work just a little bit harder to sell themselves to employers and will have to make more effort tracking down vacancies. As Andrew Mair, Director of Mercury Asset Management, commented, graduates who take time out after their degree 'need to be more creative in packaging themselves' when approaching employers.

6 Admissions Tutors' Views

University admissions tutors generally are very positive about students who are planning to take a year out before university or college of higher education. Students must, however, explain why they have decided to take time out, what they will do and what they hope to achieve. This should be fully explained on the Universities and Colleges Admissions Service (UCAS) application form. Like employers, admissions tutors are also impressed by the experience and maturity which a job, study abroad, travel or voluntary service can bring.

If you are intending to take a year out prior to higher education, it is a good idea to check the views of the admissions tutors at the institutions to which you intend to apply before sending off your UCAS application form. In general, you will find that most institutions welcome and encourage students to take a year out.

To give you an idea of what some admissions tutors think about the idea of a year out, 25 admissions tutors, who select for a variety of degree courses including maths, engineering, computer science, law, business studies, nursing, radiography, medicine, physiotherapy and humanities, were asked a series of questions. Their answers, below, will give you some idea of how universities view a year out, but bear in mind that the responses come from only a small number of admissions tutors.

1) What are your views regarding students who are planning to take a year out?

General admissions: We do not discriminate either for or against these students. They are treated equally with standard applicants.

Electrical and electronic engineering: Generally, we would encourage students to take a year out before coming to university.

Humanities: Generally favourable.
Business studies: Very positive. Students will have an opportunity to mature and develop disciplines necessary to follow a degree course.
Maths: I don't mind at all but *I would advise them to do something to stop their maths getting too rusty.*
Law: It is a good idea if useful experiences are undertaken.
Medicine: We very much welcome applications from such students; due to the length of medical training it might be advisable.
Medicine: We encourage students to take a gap year.
Computer science: For some, it is a good idea as it broadens their outlook; for others it could lead to forgetting what study demands.
Maths and statistics: It usually seems to be a very positive decision by a student to do so. Formally, they are treated just like everybody else in the admissions process.
Radiography: In favour.
Physiotherapy: Good idea.
Nursing: Usually positive, depending on the student's plans and rationale for so doing.

2) What types of experience do you value?

General admissions: A year abroad or work related to the eventual degree.

We value experiences that are relevant to the degree or of general value.

We value experiences that will broaden the mind, extend life experience and assist with their chosen course.

We accept without question applicants who wish to defer.

Anything that is positive. This could be a year in work but a period of genuine character-building travel/experiences can be equally valuable.

Experiences that will broaden their character and their outlook on life, or enable them to learn another language are considered worthwhile. We accept that some students will want to accumulate some savings with the current student grant situation. We also look favourably on experiences that are course-related. Applicants need to have an aim, a plan and should try to achieve their objectives.

Law: Anything which provides maturing experience; going round the world is better than making tea in a solicitors' office.

Computer science: We do not usually mind, although some experiences such as learning to programme a computer might be more helpful than others, eg being a waiter in a café.

Electrical and electronic engineering: The fact of being away from school, or college, is a good experience in itself particularly if it means that the student is financially independent. A placement in an engineering company is clearly more beneficial in introducing a student to the problems and rewards in industry than working in a shop.

Medicine: Certain experiences would obviously enhance a student's application, eg work placement in a medical field. However, we accept that candidates take a year out for many different reasons all of which might be valid. We value any experiences involving contact with people.

Physiotherapy: We like experiences that involve patient contact, care or voluntary work.

Nursing: We recommend voluntary work/work experience which develops initiative, responsibility, broadens horizons and insights. Also work that develops life experiences, presents a challenge, and overseas work experience.

3) Are there any experiences that you do not rate very highly?

Admissions tutors generally had the following to say.

Purely self-indulgent time filling.

Unemployment – there is a lot of scope for voluntary work in the UK and overseas.

Spending a great deal of time at home unconstructively will not benefit applicants.

We would not be very impressed with a candidate who wished to take a year out just to laze around and recover from A-levels. Apart from that, we find most experiences are beneficial in helping a candidate to achieve a different perspective on life.

Obviously, anything that is a waste of time.

Time spent drifting, unplanned, unmotivated.

Anything that will not broaden horizons and/or is not challenging.

4) What do you expect students to write on their UCAS application form?

Their plans and their rationale – briefly.

A brief statement of what they intend to do and why.

What they plan to do – why and how – and what they hope to gain.

How they will benefit from the gap year.

The truth!

5) Do you notice any difference in attitude to those who go straight from school/college to university?

Yes, they have a greater degree of self-confidence and maturity.

They are usually much more mature.

Mature students are more willing to contribute in class.

They know what they want to do and have purpose.

Yes, it is often an advantage to dissociate the 'leaving home' and 'going to university' stages. A student who has taken a year out is less likely to spend too much time drinking and socialising because he/she suddenly has the freedom to do so. Also, a student who is only going to university because it is the expected next step may realise that there are other options.

This differs greatly. Some are no different and some have achieved a greater maturity as a result of the situations that they have experienced. It seems to depend very much on the individual and what exactly they do during their year out.

Obviously, they have different experiences to bring to the course.

We hope that they are more self-reliant, mature, confident, organised, etc.

Generally, a broader perspective.

6) Are there any disadvantages to taking a year out?

Occasional problems in returning to formal study.

Not usually, provided the year is used positively.

Sometimes students may forget what they have studied before and have lack of practice with study skills. Motivation should overcome this.

Students may forget what study demands.

None.

It is particularly disadvantageous for certain subjects, eg maths, where we find that students very quickly drop from the standard they achieved at A-level. This, of course, is also true of languages unless the student takes a year out to spend it in the country of the language they wish to study. Another worry is that, once students have stopped the intensive studying they have been so used to, they tend to 'get out of the habit'.

Yes, students can forget a lot (eg maths) in one year. They should try to keep in touch with their studies.

Not unless the student has 'wasted' the year.

Returning to study can be a culture shock.

Obviously, some may find it harder to slip back into an ordered work routine.

7) How do students cope with getting back into study?

See comments in 6).

We are not aware of any serious problems.

Usually very well although there may be a short period of readjustment where help from tutors is advisable.

Some may find it difficult as they have lost momentum but, overall, we have not been overly discouraged by students' performances.

They may have some initial difficulties but the transition to university life is difficult for all students.

They rarely have any problems.

We have no evidence of any problems.

Usually quite well.

The view from UCAS

Tony Higgins, Chief Executive of UCAS, gives the following advice.

'I would recommend taking time out to prospective students. However, they need to make sure that they do something constructive and worthwhile in their year, and gain useful experience and new life skills. Course-related work and voluntary experience is particularly useful, but adventurous travel, working holidays and study abroad all contribute to broadening horizons and the development of confidence and communication skills.

To those students who will return to a scientific, engineering or maths-related course, I would suggest that they spend some time looking at their A-level notes before the start of their university course. Students can find that their memory of maths and science fades quickly.

If you are considering taking a year out, contact the admissions tutors for the courses that interest you before filling in your UCAS form. You will then be able to ascertain their views. When applying through UCAS, you will need to say what you are planning to do in your time out and what you are aiming to achieve.'

In conclusion

Many admissions tutors welcome applications from people who are planning a year out. They do, however, need convincing that the time out will be spent usefully and that the applicant will either gain further life experience or relevant work experience.

Do research the views of the admissions tutors at the institutions you are interested in before applying to UCAS. This is of particular importance to students considering degrees in subjects which include a large element of maths or science. Some, but definitely not all, maths admissions tutors may be a little wary of students taking a year out as they can forget a lot of work covered at A-level. Also, in rare cases, you may find some admissions tutors ask for higher grades from students taking a year out.

Overall, however, the message from admissions tutors regarding time out is very positive. They need to be convinced, though, that you will spend your year constructively and that you will achieve something worthwhile.

2

Taking Time Out in the UK

7 Paid Employment in the UK

If you are intending to spend your time out in paid employment in the UK, then you will have a variety of options to consider. These include:

- employment in your local area
- employment away from home
- employment related to your future career.

PAID EMPLOYMENT IN YOUR LOCAL AREA

There are a number of jobs, which you could consider locally, which will not usually require any previous experience or relevant qualifications. For details of vacancies, call into your local careers office and Jobcentre and look at adverts in your local paper. Jobs which you could think about include:

- working in a hotel as a receptionist, chamberperson, kitchen assistant, waiter/waitress, porter, catering assistant, cleaner or bar staff (expect unsociable hours and shifts)
- working in a local bar, restaurant or fast food chain such as McDonald's and Pizzaland
- working in a sports or leisure centre or social club
- industrial or domestic cleaning
- shop work
- working at a nursery, playscheme or scheme for the disabled (contact your local council for details of organisations to contact)
- working in a factory, eg as a packer, on the production line, in the warehouse or as a delivery person

- building site work, eg as a labourer
- gardening work
- office/clerical work (keyboard skills may sometimes be required)
- working in a Civil Service department or agency, or for a local council. Civil Service departments and agencies often take on casual staff to work as administrative assistants or officers. These positions can last from a few weeks to several months
- working in a hospital or residential home as a care assistant. Contact hospitals and residential homes direct – you will find addresses in *Yellow Pages*
- telephone sales and market research (this is often commission-only so make sure that your outlays do not exceed your earnings). This can be lucrative if you are good at it!

Whatever you decide to try, you need to plan ahead and make approaches to organisations early. For some of these jobs it is a good idea to sign on with local agencies, eg for office/clerical, warehouse, catering and cleaning work. When you sign on with an agency and make speculative applications, you will need a comprehensive and up-to-date CV which should be word processed. You will find that it is sometimes possible to get seasonal work in the summer holidays, or at Christmas; this is particularly true of shop work. If you can, get a part-time job in one of the above areas before your time out and then try to negotiate more hours.

PAID EMPLOYMENT AWAY FROM HOME

You may want to consider working away from home for a longer period of time. In this section, you will find details of a variety of employment opportunities such as working on children's summer camps and farms, at sports activity centres, holiday parks and villages, animal wildlife and theme parks, at stately homes, stables, hotels, motorway service stations, as au pairs and mother's helps and at English language schools. Something really different to consider would be a Short Service Commission in the army. In some cases previous experience will not be required, in others experience or a qualification will be essential.

Pay varies from organisation to organisation and can range from £30–£180 a week. The better-paid jobs are usually those for which experience or a qualification are necessary. Most organisations recruit for the busy summer months between June and September, some will require staff from as early as April to stay until October and others offer year-long employment. Accommodation is often provided and, for the lower paid jobs, meals are generally free. Read on for details of opportunities available.

Work as an au pair, nanny or mother's help

These jobs are often advertised in *The Lady* magazine and there are also au pair agencies which place au pairs with families in the UK. For many jobs you will need to be over 18.

Avalon Agency

The Avalon Agency arranges au pair placements for 25 hours a week. Pocket money, food and accommodation are provided in return for light housework and childcare as per international agreements.

For more information, contact Avalon Agency, 53 Station Road, Shalford, Guildford, Surrey GU4 8HA (telephone: 01483 63640).

Helping Hands Agency

This agency places au pairs/mother's helps in the UK (and throughout Europe and in Canada). Applicants should have at least basic childcare experience. Work is for three months during the summer or a minimum of six months at other times of the year. Applicants should be 17–27. Pocket money starts at £30–£35 per week for au pairs. Full board is provided and au pairs work five hours a day, five days a week and may do some babysitting up to two evenings a week. Mother's helps work full-time and hours are negotiated with the family. Pay ranges from £70–£120 per week depending on duties and the arrangements made with the family.

For more information, please send an SAE for a brochure and application form to Helping Hands Agency, 10 Hertford Road, Newbury Park, Ilford, Essex IG2 7HQ (telephone: 01702 602067).

Home from Home

Home from Home places au pairs with families in continental Europe and the UK. The minimum age accepted is 18 and au pairs must be prepared to stay a minimum of six months, except in the summer when they may work for 2–3 months.

For more information, contact Home from Home, Walnut Orchard, Chearsley, Aylesbury, Buckinghamshire HP18 0DA (telephone and fax: 01844 208561).

Working as a classroom assistant

Vacancies for classroom assistants and assistant matrons may sometimes be available in private preparatory schools. One organisation that may have notice of vacancies is Gabbitas Educational Consultants Ltd. School-leavers can register with the Gabbitas Staff Recruitment Department for general classroom assistant posts in preparatory schools. There are also opportunities to work in a non-teaching capacity as assistant matrons or assistant house staff.

For more information, contact Gabbitas Educational Consultants Ltd, Broughton House, 6–8 Sackville Street, Piccadilly, London W1X 2BR (telephone: 0171-734 0161).

Teaching English as a foreign language

A number of language schools recruit teachers of English as a foreign language for summer and some Easter courses. A TEFL qualification, such as the RSA Certificate, is usually required. (See the section on TEFL qualifications in chapter 10.) Some organisations also require applicants to have a degree. Most vacancies are for courses that run during July and August. They are spread around the country and include places such as Bournemouth, Brighton, Cambridge, London, Oxford and Reading. In some schools, it is possible to work as an activity organiser or sports instructor if you are not qualified to teach. Schools that recruit EFL teachers include the following.

Anglo Studies
3 Loveridge Mews
London NW6 2DP
Telephone: 0171-328 8822

Takes on EFL staff mainly for summer courses at centres throughout the UK. RSA Certificate usually required plus experience.

Anglo World Education (UK) Limited
Head Office
130–136 Poole Road
Bournemouth
Dorset BH4 9EF
Telephone: 01202 752288

Runs courses in Bournemouth, Cambridge, London, Oxford and Reading.

British Educational Language Consultants
3 St Stephen's Road
Bournemouth
Dorset BH2 6JL
Telephone: 01202 556888

EFL teachers required with degree and EFL qualification/experience.

EF Language Travel
1 Farman Street
Hove
East Sussex BN3 1AL
Telephone: 01273 723651

Recruits course directors, course leaders and teachers to teach English to French, Italian and Spanish children in London and south-east centres. Wages by arrangement, six days a week. Previous experience is required.

The Elizabeth Johnson Organisation Ltd
West House
19–21 West Street
Haslemere
Surrey GU27 2AE
Telephone: 01428 652751

Runs summer and Easter language courses mainly in the south of England. Most of the teachers employed are qualified (PGCE, BEd or TEFL) though there are some openings for graduates (preferably with a modern language degree and/or TEFL experience). There are also a few vacancies for people to organise activities and excursions. No specific qualifications are required although sporting interests are desirable.

Euro-Academy
77a George Street
Croydon
Surrey CR0 1LD
Telephone: 0181-681 2905

Employs temporary EFL teachers for Easter and summer courses; mainly employs graduates with EFL qualification.

International Community School
4 York Terrace East
Regent's Park
London NW1 4PT
Telephone: 0171-935 1206

Summer EFL staff employed, mainly graduates with RSA Certificate.

International Study (IS)
The Manor
Hazleton
Cheltenham
Gloucestershire GL54 4EB
Telephone: 01451 860379

Takes on EFL teachers all year round for summer, autumn and Easter courses. Teachers are mainly graduates with the RSA Certificate and a minimum of one year's EFL experience (those with a PGCE may not need experience). Contact IS for an application form.

Nord Anglia International Limited
10 Eden Place
Cheadle
Cheshire SK8 1AT
Telephone: 0161-491 4191

Contact at the beginning of the year for information on vacancies.

Oxford Intensive School of English (Youth Language Centres)
OISE House
Binsey Lane
Oxford OX2 0EY
Telephone: 01865 249218

Runs a few Easter and a number of summer language courses in the south of England. Requires TEFL teachers and leisure directors; applicants should be graduates with an RSA Certificate. Apply in January for a brochure.

Padworth College
Padworth
Reading
Berkshire RG7 4NR
Telephone: 01734 832644

Contact in January for more details on vacancies.

Regent Summer Schools
19–23 Oxford Street (3rd floor)
London W1R 1RF
Telephone: 0171-734 1137

Contact in January for more information on vacancies.

Victoria School of English
28 Graham Terrace
Sloane Square
London SW1
Telephone: 0171-730 1333

Temporary EFL staff required from June to September. Degree plus RSA Certificate required.

Working with children on holiday camps

A number of organisations recruit people to work on children's summer camps and at activity centres. A variety of staff is needed such as bar staff, general assistants, shop and catering staff, office workers as well as children's activity organisers, group leaders, walk leaders and sports instructors. Instructors usually need to possess qualifications in, for example, tennis, swimming, archery, fell-walking, rock climbing, windsurfing, sailing or riding.

Action Holidays Ltd

About 200 staff are needed to run multi-activity centres for children aged 5–15 in the London area, Cheshire, Staffordshire and Lancashire. Supervisors are responsible for co-ordinating children's care; instructors are also needed for a wide range of sports activities.

For more information, contact Action Holidays Ltd, Robinwood, Jumps Road, Todmorden, Lancashire OL14 8HJ (telephone: 01706 814554).

Ardmore Adventure Ltd

Leaders and supervisors needed for adventure residential camps, for 5–16 year olds, located throughout the UK. Board and lodging are provided, plus wages from £45 per week, depending on hours worked.

For more information, contact Operations Manager, Ardmore Adventure Ltd, 11–15 High Street, Marlow, Buckinghamshire SL7 1AU (telephone: 01628 890060).

Camp Beaumont

Residential camps need group leaders with experience to plan, organise and supervise children's activities. Free board and lodging are provided and group leaders are paid £50 per week. Monitors are required to supervise transportation of children at the camps.

For more information, contact Recruitment Manager, Camp Beaumont, Bridge House, Orchard Lane, Huntingdon, Cambridgeshire PE18 6QT (telephone: 01480 456123).

Freetime Summer Camps

Activity holidays organised for children aged 4–15 at day centres in Surrey. Sports instructors and counsellors are needed between July and August and are paid from £75 upwards per week for a five to seven day week. Activities include archery, arts and crafts, canoeing, rifle shooting, tennis and windsurfing.

For more information, contact Freetime Summer Camps, Park House, Moor Lane, Woking, Surrey GU22 9RB (telephone: 01483 740242).

Freetime Watersports Centres

Instructors of windsurfing, canoeing and sailing needed for two watersports centres, in Berkshire and Surrey, from April to October. Applicants should have acquired governing body instructor qualifications. Pay from £95 a week upwards.

For more information, contact Freetime Summer Camps (details above).

HF Holidays Ltd

HF Holidays is the world's largest walking and special interest holiday company. In Britain, it runs 19 country house hotels situated in national parks and areas of outstanding natural beauty. It needs three types of applicants: walk leaders, children's activity leaders and hotel staff.

Walk leaders and children's activity leaders are paid £15 per week plus board and lodging (students are paid £40 per week plus board and lodging). Age range 18–65. Walk leaders need experience plus excellent map and compass ability. Successful applicants can work from two weeks to 30 weeks a year. Apply early as residential assessment takes place between Christmas and Easter.

Children's activity leaders are needed for July and August each year to organise and supervise children's games and activities.

For its many country guest houses, which are located throughout England, Scotland and Wales, HF Holidays recruits staff for the following positions.

Assistant management: Responsible to management for efficient organisation and smooth function of all household duties. Experience essential.

General assistants: For domestic work in household and dining room. Training provided.

Kitchen porters: To assist cooks with the cleaning of utensils and maintaining cleanliness of kitchen. Involves the preparation of vegetables and salads. Training given.
Assistant cooks: Previous experience preferable though positions are suitable for students undertaking first appointments after college.
Deputy cooks: Practical experience required. Responsible for the kitchen in the head cook's absence.
Head cooks: Practical experience of catering for up to 100 covers is essential.

Rates of pay vary from £50–£180 per week depending on the position. For more information, contact HF Holidays Ltd, Redhills, Penrith, Cumbria CA11 0DT (telephone: 01768 67676 for walk leaders and children's representatives and 01768 899988 for hotel staff).

PGL Young Adventure Ltd
PGL Young Adventure is Europe's largest provider of activity courses for children and has been offering work in the outdoors to young people for nearly 40 years. Each year PGL takes on approximately 3,000 people to work in its centres in Britain and France. The first centres open in February and continue to operate until October, while the heaviest staffing requirements fall between May and September. Priority is given to applicants who can start in May. There are also limited vacancies just for July and August.

Vacancies exist for the following.

Instructors: Teach a variety of outdoor activities such as sailing, canoeing, rafting, surfing, safety-boat driving, rowing, swimming, pony-trekking, archery, fencing, judo, hill-walking, climbing, abseiling, caving, orienteering, assault course and raft-building. During July and August, there are limited vacancies for ball sports, racquet sports and for teachers of arts and crafts, drama and video film-making. Possession of instructor qualifications will enhance your chances of employment. PGL also runs instructor training courses.

Group leaders: Care for the children outside the main activity hours. Group leaders take responsibility for a group of children throughout their stay at the centre and act as friend, teacher, parent and counsellor. Group leaders also organise evening entertainments. Previous experience of working with children is required, minimum age is 20. During the school holidays a number of travelling courier/group leaders are employed. Couriers accompany children on trips to various parts of Europe; a sound knowledge of at least one foreign European language is required.
Support staff: Cooks, catering staff, nurses, drivers, administrative assistants, domestic assistants, site/stores assistants, night security staff, tuck shop/bar assistants and maintenance staff. For some of these positions, previous experience is required.

Applicants need to be at least 18 years old, unless applying specifically to work in France or as a group leader for which the minimum age is 20. If you work for more than one season, you may be able to progress to a senior post.

All posts are residential; food and accommodation are provided plus pocket money ranging from £30–£47 per week, depending on start date and length of service.

In addition to the jobs mentioned above, PGL also has limited vacancies for Saturday couriers, ski resort representatives, TEFL tutors, French tutors, eastern Europe tour couriers and study visit organisers in France.

For more information, contact Seasonal Personnel Department, PGL Young Adventure Ltd, Alton Court, Penyard Lane, Ross-on-Wye, Herefordshire HR9 5NR (telephone: 01989 767833).

Working in the tourist industry

There is a wide variety of work available in the tourist industry in the UK, from working as a sports instructor at a holiday centre to assisting the warden in a youth hostel.

Working at holiday centres

These centres need a variety of staff to work with children and adults. There are jobs for bar staff, cleaners, waiting staff, clerical assistants, receptionists, sports instructors and entertainers.

Bourne Leisure Group Ltd

This company owns over 20 holiday parks in the UK. Receptionists, bar staff, lifeguards, site workers and children's entertainers are required. Minimum age 18.

For more information, contact Bourne Leisure Group Ltd, Normandy Court, 1 Wolsey Road, Hemel Hempstead, Hertfordshire HP2 4TU (telephone: 01442 244006).

Butlins

Butlins recruits staff, such as bar staff, cleaners, cooks, waiting staff, children's supervisors, to work from May to October in its holiday centres.

For more information, contact Butlins, Personnel Department, South Coast World, Bognor Regis, West Sussex PO21 1JJ (telephone: 01243 860709).

Countrywide Holidays Association

Countrywide Holidays Association hires general assistants at a weekly rate, plus free board and lodging. Duties include domestic work and previous experience is an advantage. Minimum employment is for six months.

For more information, contact Countrywide Holidays Association, Birch Heys, Cromwell Range, Manchester M14 6HU (telephone: 0161-225 1000).

Haven Leisure Ltd

A variety of opportunities is available. For more details, contact Haven Leisure Ltd, Swan Court, Waterhouse Street, Hemel Hempstead, Hertfordshire HP1 1DS (telephone: 01442 230300).

Pontins

Pontins requires bar staff, cleaners, cooks, waiters and children's supervisors from May to October in its holiday centres.

For more information, contact Pontins, PO Box 100, Sagar House, The Green, Eccleston, Chawle, Lancashire PR7 5QQ (telephone: 01257 452452).

Warner Holidays Ltd

Holiday villages and hotels for adults only throughout the UK require catering, bar, leisure, entertainment, cleaning, retail and receptionist staff. Competitive rates of pay, board and lodging for people over 18 years of age.

For more information, contact the Personnel Manager, Warner Holidays Ltd, Warner House, North Street, Havant, Hampshire PO9 1SQ (telephone: 01705 478888).

Youth Hostels Association (YHA)

Instructors are needed for YHA activity holidays plus leaders for walking tours, water sports, hillcrafts, etc, at many centres throughout England and Wales. Free board and lodging, plus a small weekly payment.

For more information, contact YHA, Trevelyan House, 8 St Stephen's Hill, St Albans, Hertfordshire AL1 2DY (telephone: 01727 855215).

Working in youth hostels

There are sometimes vacancies for people aged 18 plus to assist wardens in youth hostels. These positions are usually filled by the spring, so enquire early in the year, or late in the year before you intend to work.

Further information about posts can be obtained by contacting the Youth Hostels Association, Trevelyan House, 8 St Stephen's Hill, St Albans, Hertfordshire AL1 2DY (telephone: 01727 855215).

Working in a hotel

You could apply for positions in hotels anywhere in the country since it is often possible to 'live in'. Positions available include those for cooks, catering assistants, bar staff, stewards, cleaners and waiting staff.

Friendly Hotels plc

Waiting staff, room cleaners, bar staff and stewards are required, to work a 39-hour, five-day week. The minimum age is 18; board and lodging are often available.

For more information, contact Friendly Hotels plc, Premier House, 10 Greycoat Place, London, SW1P 1SB (telephone: 0171-222 8866).

Little Chef

Catering assistants needed for catering establishments throughout the UK. Contact your local restaurant regarding vacancies.

Welcome Break

Part of the Forte Group. For information regarding vacancies, contact the Personnel Officer, Forte Welcome Break Ltd, M1 Motorway, Newport Pagnell, Bucks, MK16 8DS (telephone: 01908 217722).

And now for something completely different

For a challenging and rewarding job before starting university, you may want to consider a short spell in the army. Below, you will find details of Short Service Limited Commissions.

The Army Short Service Limited Commissions Scheme

Each year about 40 young men and women, waiting to go to university, are offered Short Service Limited Commissions in the army. They serve from four to 18 months as officers in regular units, and have no further liability. For 1995/6 a salary of £10,010 rising to £10,694 after nine months is paid to those on the 18-month commission, together with a uniform allowance. Applicants must have reached the age of 18 years and be under 20 years on the day of commissioning, and must have already gained a university place. The closing dates for applications are 31 September for those starting in January, and 30 June for an October start.

A student who took part in the scheme wrote that it was:

'Not a recruiting effort, only a public relations exercise, ie to disseminate a sympathetic attitude to the army in university and beyond. After only a month's very rushed training, I was in Germany and soon fulfilling a normal junior officer's job, ie administering a troop of three tanks and the crew of 11 men besides myself. Although it is not the life for me, I enjoyed the responsibility and the complete break from academic pursuits. The scheme is financially very rewarding, valuable in terms of experiences, and entails no commitment to the army during, or after, university.'

For more information, contact Directorate of Army Recruiting, Ministry of Defence, DARID, Room 1125, Empress State Building, London SW6 1TR (telephone: 0171-824 3272).

EMPLOYMENT RELATED TO YOUR FUTURE CAREER

If you intend to work in the UK, perhaps the best way to spend your time is gaining experience in the area of work that, in the long-term, you want to enter. Excellent experience can be gained through voluntary work, but you may also be keen to consider relevant paid employment. This type of employment is, however, not the easiest to find – not least because popular fields of work such as journalism and the media do not often have short-term vacancies – so be prepared to spend a lot of time contacting organisations speculatively.

Some companies take on students for vacation work but competition for positions is fierce. You will have to apply early and put in a good application. You will need to *sell* yourself. The more personal qualities, keyboard, computing and language skills you have, the more you will impress an employer. One good way of getting a foot in the door of a company is to develop your office skills and get a job as an office junior or administrator. You will then get the opportunity to impress and you will gain an understanding about the industry concerned. If you do manage to get a vacation post in the area of work you want to enter, your CV will stand out from others when applying for permanent jobs later. Those of you trying to gain experience in a popular area of work may have to be content with a period of unpaid work experience. Even this, though, looks good on a CV as it shows drive and initiative.

There are some organisations, such as The Year in Industry and Towers Perrin, which recruit gap-year students who want to gain experience in industry during their year out. You will find their details below.

The Year in Industry

This scheme matches bright young men and women, who wish to spend a year in industry before starting a degree course, with companies who have useful work for them to undertake. It offers students a first-hand insight into industry, giving them a head start in their degree course and their career. Paid work in the company is backed by 20+ days of off-the-job training to develop practical and interpersonal skills and business awareness.

The Year in Industry is open to any student interested in making a career in industry, whatever degree course they are taking, but it is especially suited to those interested in engineering, science and technology – subjects for which there is an acknowledged shortage of candidates. Of 800 applicants to the scheme in 1993, 345 were placed, of whom 25 were non-technical – a reflection of the demands of industry.

The Year in Industry is available right across England and Wales, through a network of regional centres. Applications should be made as early as possible in the final year of A-levels/BTEC/Advanced GNVQ/Highers. Students are paid the employer's 'going rate' subject to a recommended minimum of £120 per week. Those who live away from home are responsible for their own accommodation. The programme runs from August to July.

Some quotes from former students with The Year in Industry include:

> ‘I found that The Year in Industry scheme offered invaluable industrial experience and is well worth the effort for the employer and student alike. I would therefore recommend the scheme particularly to any student who is contemplating a career in engineering or related subjects. I couldn’t have done without it.’

> ‘During the placement you do a real job with all the responsibilities and challenges.’

> ‘The skills I have gained this year will benefit me through university and into the future. I had many fears about entering the workplace, but I am sure that I have emerged a more confident and employable person.’

> ‘I will leave with many skills, and with the ability to communicate more confidently through a wider variety of media.’

Tim Courtney

The Year in Industry case-study

In the first year of his A-levels, Tim decided that he needed a break from study before going on to do chemical engineering at university.

‘My school told me about The Year in Industry which offered a chance of one year’s work experience. Early in my second year of A-levels, I applied for a placement with a chemical engineering company. In August I went for an interview at a chemical firm in Liverpool but it wasn’t really what I was looking for so I turned the offer down. I did a labouring job for a while and then, in November, I was offered a placement with London Underground's Engineering Training and Personnel Department. If I had been more flexible about the branch of engineering I wanted, I think I would have been offered a placement sooner and it might have been more directly relevant to my degree.

I spent eight hectic months with London Underground. The salary, equivalent to £9,000 per annum, was reasonable. One of my main achievements was overhauling the administrative systems which London Underground uses for its trainee engineers – 96 of them at any one time. I arranged meetings with the trainees to find out how they felt the systems could be improved. I also dealt with the trainees' mentors to find out what they thought of the training programme and what they expected from their trainees. After this research, I drew up some proposals and was pleased when they were implemented by London Underground. I also helped with the day-to-day activities of the department booking training courses and dealing with trainees' general enquiries.

The placement was varied and challenging and I was sent on a number of really useful training courses: personnel selection tests, communication and interpersonal skills, presentation skills, training needs' analysis and interviewing skills. I developed a lot of transferable skills through working in a team, writing business letters, working in an office environment and meeting new people.

In the long term, my plan is to become a chartered engineer and the experience I gained at London Underground will help me to get incorporated status with the Institution of Chemical Engineers. Normally, this takes two years after a degree but it will only take me 18 months as the Institute recognises personnel experience. My placement has also given me an idea of what selectors look for in trainees, what tests are used and how training schemes are run which will be helpful when I apply for jobs. And, of course, I will also be able to ask London Underground for a reference.

The Year in Industry is ideal for people looking for a challenge. As well as useful work experience, you also get to make friends in the industry you are aiming for. However, if you are going on to do a scientific, maths or engineering course, you will need to re-visit your A-level work to make the transition to university study easier. During my year out, I tried to stop my maths getting rusty by going through a book of mathematics problems. ❜

For more information on The Year in Industry, contact The Year in Industry, National Director, University of Manchester, Simon Building, Oxford Road, Manchester M13 9PL (telephone: 0161-275 4396).

Towers Perrin

Towers Perrin is an international firm of consulting actuaries and management consultants. It offers gap-year employment from 1 September until mid-May of the following year to students wishing to take a year out between study at 18 and higher education.

Gap-year students will work in the Property Casualty Unit, the general insurance actuarial consulting division. The work will appeal to students with a strong interest in maths and computing and applicants should expect to gain a high grade at A-level maths or the equivalent.

Towers Perrin will provide valuable hands-on experience working in a financial consultancy in the heart of London together with in-depth computer training. The job is rewarding both financially and intellectually (no tea-making!).

To apply, please contact Clare Desmond at Towers Perrin, Castlewood House, 77–91 New Oxford Street, London WC1A 1PX (telephone: 0171-379 4000/4411). Apply in October/November of your final year of A-levels/Advanced GNVQ/BTEC/Highers, etc.

Sponsorship

Some firms offer sponsorships to students and expect them to work for the firm during their vacations and often after completion of their degree. Sponsorships are mainly available for students of engineering, science, computing and other technical areas. There are also a few sponsorships available for those taking business and financial degrees. See Part 5 for sources of information on sponsorships.

8 Work in the Community

A period of voluntary work in the community can be extremely rewarding and can be beneficial in that it develops maturity, self-awareness and a sense of responsibility. There is much scope for voluntary work in the UK ranging from working on social projects with the mentally or physically disabled, people with special needs, the elderly, children or the homeless to domestic work and campaigning. Previous experience is usually not required as volunteers generally work with, or are guided by, experienced staff.

The minimum age for projects is often 18 but, in some cases, organisations will accept 16 or 17 year olds. A few organisations set a maximum age; this can be 25, 30 or 35. Projects vary in length from a few weeks to a year or more. Quite a number of organisations set a minimum period of service at six months. All organisations expect a high degree of commitment from volunteers. Board and lodging are usually provided and a number of organisations pay volunteers pocket money which is often £20–£30 a week. Sometimes volunteers are expected to pay their own travel expenses; in other cases these can be claimed back. Accommodation varies. Some volunteers live-in in a residential home or the home of the person they are looking after; others are accommodated in hall of residence-type accommodation. Some volunteers will need to be prepared for fairly basic accommodation and may have to share a room.

Some of the voluntary projects mentioned in this chapter (and in chapter 9) are workcamps. Workcamps are communities where volunteers work together on a social or environmental project and take it in turns to do the cooking and cleaning. Accommodation is often shared and can be basic. Workcamps attract people from all over the world. Some of the benefits of a communal setting are that you meet lots of new people and the social life can be good.

Below, you will find details of organisations offering voluntary opportunities in the UK. Many organisations that work in the community are Christian in their philosophy. These have been listed separately for those of you who will feel more comfortable in a broadly Christian working environment.

Christian-based organisations

Careforce

Careforce serves evangelical churches and organisations, throughout the UK and the Republic of Ireland, by placing Christian volunteers (aged 18–23) where their help is most needed. Careforce enables volunteers to offer themselves to serve God in an area of need and to share fully in the life of a Christian community.

Placements include serving with local churches, youth and schools work, evangelistic outreach, and helping people who are homeless, elderly, have drug/alcohol-related problems, have a physical disability or learning difficulties, or are from families facing difficulties.

All Careforce volunteers are provided with their board and lodging plus weekly pocket money. The Careforce year begins in September and lasts for 10–12 months with volunteers being placed according to their gifts, skills, experience and abilities. In September 1994, 117 volunteers were placed by Careforce.

Interviews, for placements starting the following September, are held from January through to August.

For further details and an application form, contact Philip McAleese, Recruitment Co-ordinator, 577 Kingston Road, London SW20 8SA (telephone: 0181-543 8671).

Church Missionary Society (CMS)

Britain Experience Placements are for those in the 18–30 age range and provide opportunities for young people to gain experience of a part of Britain that is culturally different from what they are used to. Placements are for

6–18 months. CMS provides the cost of training and pays living expenses and pocket money, but participants are responsible for other costs.

For more information, contact the Experience Programme Adviser, Partnership House, CMS, 157 Waterloo Road, London SE1 8UU (telephone: 0171-928 8681).

The Corrymeela Community

Corrymeela is an ecumenical community committed to the work of reconciliation in Ireland and beyond. Volunteers on the Serve and Learn programme work at the Community's centre on the North Antrim coast at Ballycastle. They undertake domestic and manual work in running the centre as well as being directly involved with the wide variety of groups that use the centre.

A balance is sought of young adults, aged 18–30, from Ireland and overseas who are willing to live in a demanding community setting, and are able to relate to a wide range of people from different backgrounds. The Community seeks people who can handle responsibility and are willing to be flexible. Applicants who have an active Christian commitment to the work of reconciliation are preferred.

Ten volunteers are required for one-year positions beginning in September and two volunteers are needed for six months beginning in March. There are also summer voluntary programmes lasting three weeks. Those interested should apply by the end of February for the one-year positions, by the end of October/November for the six-months positions and by the end of April for the summer positions. A room and board are provided for volunteers and those who volunteer for six months or a year are paid £20 a week pocket money. All volunteers share twin rooms in a staff house.

For more information, contact the Volunteer Co-ordinator, Corrymeela Community, 5 Drumaroan Road, Ballycastle, County Antrim BT54 6QU (telephone: 012657 62626/62119).

Jesuit Volunteer Communities (JVC) Britain

JVC offers young adults (18–35) a year of living in lay communities while working in an area of social need. Volunteers live in communities of five or six, in inner city areas of Birmingham, Glasgow, Liverpool and Manchester, and work in a variety of placements organised by JVC and other agencies. Placements include working with people who are homeless, those with mental health problems, learning difficulties and victims of crime. Volunteers receive rent, bill and food allowances and pocket money.

JVC offers a Development Programme, which all volunteers attend. The JVC year begins in August with a six-day orientation and introduction. The programme continues with a weekend in November on community, a communal retreat in February, a weekend in May on social justice, and finishes with evaluation in mid-August.

Volunteers should be able to commit themselves to one year of service and need to have a wish to live in a community, a desire to live simply, a willingness to explore personal and Ignatian spirituality (a means of reflection on experience, life and social justice) and a commitment to work for justice.

For more information, contact Promotion and Recruitment Co-ordinator, JVC Britain, St Wilfrid's Enterprise Centre, Royce Road, Hulme, Manchester M15 5BJ (telephone: 0161-226 6717).

Team on Missions

The Department of Youth and Children's Work requires four volunteers to work together in its Team on Missions throughout Ireland in youth groups, church activities and summer programmes. The team year begins on 1 September for a 12-month period, with the possible option of a further year. Accommodation, expenses and pocket money are provided.

For more information, contact Reverend D G Neilands, General Secretary, Irish Methodist Youth

Department, Aldersgate House, University Road, Belfast BT7 1NA (telephone: 01232 327191).

Time for God (TFG)

TFG places young people (17–25 years) in Christian projects throughout the UK and, once 'matched', ensures the volunteers receive regular support and back-up to enable them to get the most from the experience – this is through regular visits from full-time staff, residential training conferences and frequent contact by phone and letter. Volunteers must either have their own Christian faith, or be actively seeking/exploring Christianity.

Placements involve volunteers becoming part of the staff teams in their placement – whether this is a children's home, a community centre, activity project or a church. The project covers a huge range of client groups including ex-offenders, disabled children, youth groups, drug addicts, the homeless, the elderly and children and families coping with HIV/AIDS.

No qualifications are required. TFG will try to make the most of any skills you have. Each placement is unique in terms of what is required from the volunteer and in the benefits the volunteer gains from working there. However, the selection procedure for placements requires completion of a detailed job description and timetable, and each placement is visited by TFG staff before volunteers are suggested. Volunteers work a maximum of 35–40 hours per week with two days off, adequate supervision and support and good quality accommodation is provided. Volunteers visit the placement before either side commits itself to the arrangement. Placements are for a minimum of six months and a maximum of 12 months. There will be places for 250 volunteers in 1995/6.

For more information, contact Time for God, 2 Chester House, Pages Lane, London N10 1PR (telephone: 0181-883 1504, fax: 0181-365 2471). It is advisable to apply in writing to the scheme's office at least two months before the planned start date (September or January).

Toc H

Toc H is a Christian society, originally founded to combat loneliness and hatred and to encourage Christian comradeship among British soldiers after World War I, that now engages in a wide range of social work in the English-speaking world.

Toc H runs short-term residential projects throughout the year lasting from a weekend up to three weeks. Most of these are in Britain and include working with disabled people, children in need, on playschemes and camps and on conservation projects. Toc H also runs projects in Germany where volunteers work with the families of British service personnel (see chapter 12 in Part 3).

The minimum age is 16, and 18 for some projects. There is no maximum age. EU citizens are given preference. More than 500 volunteers are recruited each year. Further details can be found in the Toc H Projects' Programme, published twice yearly on the first Monday of March and September. Early application is advisable.

For more information, contact National Projects Coordinator, Toc H, 1 Forest Close, Wendover, Aylesbury, Buckinghamshire HP22 6BT (telephone: 01296 623911).

United Society for the Propagation of the Gospel (USPG)

USPG runs a root group programme in Britain which offers you the chance to form a small community with two to three other young Christians (18–30 years). You will join a church in another culture, class and area of Britain and will find ways of contributing to the life of the church and the local community.

For more information, contact United Society for the Propagation of the Gospel, Partnership House, 157 Waterloo Road, London SE1 8XA (telephone: 0171-928 8681).

Secular organisations

The Camphill Village Trust

The Trust aims to help people with mental disabilities to gain more independence and to lead more fulfilling lives.

Many of the mentally ill residents come to the Trust for assessment and rehabilitation before moving to another community. Volunteers live communally with the residents and the more permanent co-workers. The Trust runs three villages, where the residents work on the land or in workshops, two town homes and a college/assessment centre.

Volunteers should be at least 20 and the minimum length of service is six months, but preferably one year. Board, lodging and pocket money are provided. Applications are received throughout the year.

For more information, contact the Co-ordinator, Camphill Village Trust, Delrow House, Hilfield Lane, Aldenham, Watford, Hertfordshire WD2 8DJ (telephone: 01923 856006).

The Commonwealth Institute

The Commonwealth Institute offers voluntary work opportunities relating to educational programmes, the leisure industry, exhibitions and the arts. There are no age restrictions.

To apply, send CV and covering letter to the Personnel Department, The Commonwealth Institute, 230 Kensington High Street, London W8 6NQ (telephone: 0171-603 4535).

Community Service Volunteers (CSV)

CSV provides more gap-year opportunities than any other organisation in the UK. No one is rejected. Opportunities are for those aged 16–35 years, and over 50.

CSV matches the interests, experience and skills of over 3,000 volunteers with people throughout the UK who need their help – from befriending homeless young people in hostels to working alongside people with special needs. Other volunteers help people with disabilities to live independently in their own homes, or act as positive role models to other young people.

Being a CSV is an excellent way for young people to gain the maturity and independence to cope with living away from home. The challenge of becoming a CSV teaches young people a lot about themselves as well as other people. It also looks good on a CV.

For students studying areas such as medicine, nursing, social work or psychology, volunteering with CSV provides practical experience and challenges which can not be taught in the lecture theatre. Nearly all ex-CSVs say that volunteering increased their self-confidence, taught them a wide range of interpersonal skills and left them with the most poignant memories of their lives.

Every CSV is placed away from home with free board, lodgings, food and £22 a week pocket money. Accommodation varies according to the project, but is usually similar to that offered in university halls of residence.

CSVs volunteer for between four months and a year. Many gap-year volunteers stay on a project for eight or nine months, although some volunteers prefer to spend that time on two very different projects.

In 1993, Claire Brett (now 20) left school after A-levels and volunteered to work in a boarding school, run by Barnados, for 60 children with physical disabilities. She began an occupational therapy degree in 1994.

> I wanted to see the other side of life, life outside school... I have become much more confident in myself and with dealing with other people. I'm learning to cope with situations by myself and using my initiative more.

Siobhan Boyle (23) took a year out after her Law Society Finals to work with young homeless people in London.

> I've learned to deal with stressful and difficult situations in a calm and rational way. I also feel I've become more patient and a good listener... My time at the project has been very rewarding.

Marc Taylor (23) volunteered at a home for young people with learning difficulties after graduating.

> 'It's a chance to do something you probably haven't done before or will not do again. It's challenging, rewarding and has real job satisfaction.

Nikki Rea (19) volunteered to look after a lady with dementia on an Independent Living Project in 1993 before going on to study psychology at university.

> It's been very interesting and really challenging. I have found my own strengths and weaknesses and I feel I have made a big contribution to someone else's independence.

For more information, contact Community Service Volunteers, 237 Pentonville Road, London N1 9NJ (telephone: 0171-278 6601, fax: 0171-833 0149).

Glasgow Simon Community
Volunteers contact and offer friendship and practical help to men and women who have experienced long-term homelessness, especially those who sleep/have slept rough. They work in small group homes alongside ex-homeless people, sharing in group living, giving and receiving support, and taking responsibility for money and medicines.

Volunteers must be 18 years or over. Attitudes are important; the Community aims to accept people as they are, to live with them on an equal basis without patronising them. The work is demanding, so emotional stability and reasonable physical fitness are necessary. Seven volunteers are recruited anually. Applications are accepted throughout the year. The minimum length of service is six months, preferably longer.

Volunteers work a 35-hour week on a rota basis with a maximum of two sleep-overs every seven-day period (with separate living accommodation provided). They receive a weekly personal allowance, an allowance for a holiday every three months and travel expenses.

For more information, contact Volunteer Co-ordinator, Glasgow Simon Community, 69 Dixon Road, Govanhill, Glasgow G42 8AT (telephone: 0141-423 0949).

The Guide Association

Volunteers are taken on for administrative and domestic duties in connection with Guide houses both in the UK and abroad. Volunteers should hold membership of an organisation affiliated to the World Association of Girl Guides and Girl Scouts and be 18 or over. The minimum length of service is one month and there are very few vacancies available. Applications, therefore, should be made as far in advance as possible. Accommodation and pay is dependent on the type and place of the project. Travel fares are paid by the volunteer.

For more information, contact The Guide Association, 17–19 Buckingham Palace Road, London SW1W 0PT (telephone: 0171-834 6242).

Homes for Homeless People

Founded in 1970, the object of the organisation is to work on behalf of single homeless people. Volunteers must be 18 years or over. Activities include the establishment of independent Cyrenian (a group offering support to the homeless) and other groups, which organise residential community houses and make some form of basic provision for those who would otherwise sleep rough. These projects are staffed by small teams of volunteer workers who share their lives with the residents for periods of 6–12 months. Approximately 300 volunteers are recruited each year.

For more information, contact Volunteers' Secretary, Homes for Homeless People, 6 Union Street, Luton, Bedfordshire LU1 3AN (telephone: 01582 481426).

International Voluntary Service (IVS)

IVS is a voluntary organisation that exists to provide

opportunities for voluntary work for people, both in the UK and in western, central and eastern Europe, in the belief that this will further international understanding and lead to a more just and peaceful world.

IVS recruits volunteers, who are over 18, to work in about 50 workcamps in Britain and hundreds more in over 30 countries abroad. The length of a workcamp ranges from 2–4 weeks. The work carried out varies enormously and can include any of the following:

- campaigning on issues related to developing countries, racism, disarmament and peace education
- working with people with disabilities, children or the elderly, either in their own homes, at a day centre or on a holiday
- ecological and environmental work
- women's camps
- artistic/cultural camps.

The workcamp group will normally be made up of between six and 20 volunteers from at least three/four different countries. The volunteers live and work together, sharing responsibility for the organisation of the work and domestic arrangements such as cooking and cleaning. In return for the work they carry out, volunteers receive basic food and accommodation for free. Most workcamps take place between June and September but there are others running at different times of the year. You will increase your chances of getting a place on a camp if you apply early and are flexible.

Workcamps help to support communities by providing outside assistance to projects undertaking worthwhile voluntary work. At the same time, they offer opportunities for volunteers to meet new people, learn skills and have some fun. Living together in an international group, volunteers learn about different lifestyles and cultures. The experience of living in a community frequently has a marked impact on people and influences the rest of their lives.

For more information, contact one of the IVS UK offices listed below.

IVS North
Castle Hill House
21 Otley Road
Headingley
Leeds
Yorkshire LS6 3AA
Telephone: 0113 230 4600

IVS South
Old Hall
East Bergholt
Colchester
Essex CO7 6TQ
Telephone: 01206 298215

IVS Scotland
7 Upper Bow
Edinburgh EH1 2JN
Telephone: 0131-226 6722

L'Arche

L'Arche is a registered charity and L'Arche communities are places where people with learning difficulties work together in a simple way. Volunteers are needed to work in a community with people with mental disabilities. The organisation views the spiritual life of working together as being as important as material welfare.

Assistants need to be at least 18. Craft skills are useful for workshops and for domestic duties. Free board and lodging are provided, plus pocket money. Most communities ask volunteers to stay for six months, but one year is preferable. Many assistants stay on for between one and two years.

For further information, send an SAE for a booklet to L'Arche, 10 Briggate, Silsden, Keighley, West Yorkshire BD20 9JT (telephone: 01535 656186).

The Leonard Cheshire Foundation

This organisation offers voluntary work opportunities, mainly helping with the care of adults with severe physical disabilities. Volunteers should be over 18 and have a genuine concern for the disabled. Previous experience is an advantage, but not essential. A good knowledge of the English language and communication skills are needed.

The minimum length of service is two months, but few vacancies are for less than three months. Immediate vacancies are rare, so apply early leaving time for a vacancy to arise. Applicants need to state the dates they can offer and how long they are available for. About 70–80 volunteers are recruited each year.

Board and accommodation (sometimes sharing) are provided in a home, with pocket money (£27 per week, reviewed each year). Travel expenses are paid by the volunteer.

For details of the voluntary work scheme and an application form, contact the Personnel Secretary, The Leonard Cheshire Foundation, 26–29 Maunsel Street, London SW1P 2QN (telephone: 0171-828 1822).

Quaker International Social Projects (QISP)

QISP organises voluntary projects in the UK. The projects are one to three weeks in length and involve groups of volunteers, half from abroad, living and working together to meet a community need. There is a variety of projects to choose from each year such as manual work or working with disadvantaged people or with children. Experience on a project in the UK is a qualification for placement abroad.

The summer programme is published in April and it is advisable to apply early. Most places are filled by the end of June. To apply ask for an application form; a registration fee is charged.

For more information, contact Quaker International Social Projects, Friends House, Euston Road, London NW1 2BJ (telephone: 0171-387 3601).

The Sue Ryder Foundation

The Foundation serves the sick and disabled of all age groups. Most volunteers work at the Sue Ryder Home and Headquarters based at Cavendish, Suffolk and at other Sue Ryder homes. Volunteers work alongside staff, doing whatever work is necessary such as helping with the patients, domestic, office or other work. Volunteers need to be flexible and adaptable and have a strong sense of responsibility and dedication. Free meals and simple accommodation are provided plus pocket money.

The normal minimum period of service is two months, although, at times, it may be possible to consider shorter periods. Volunteers are particularly needed in the months September to June. Early application is essential for the months of July and August. Applicants must be at least 16 years old.

For more information and an application form, con tact Sue Ryder Foundation Headquarters, Cavendish, Sudbury, Suffolk CO10 8AY (telephone: 01787 280252).

Support and Housing Assistance for People with Disabilities (SHAD)

SHAD recruits full-time volunteers throughout the year, to act as 'the arms and legs' of severely physically disabled people. Volunteers provide 24-hour cover, working shifts (usually one day on, two days off), and work on a one-to-one basis with disabled tenants, thus enabling them to live independently in their own homes around south-west London. Accommodation, food allowance, pocket money and travel expenses are provided. Volunteering with SHAD provides excellent work experience in a friendly and supportive atmosphere.

About 80 placements are available each year for which no qualifications are required. The minimum length of service is four months and there is no upper limit.

For more information, contact the Support Worker, SHAD Wandsworth, The Nightingale Centre, 8 Balham Hill, London SW12 9EA (telephone: 0181-675 6095).

Winged Fellowship

Winged Fellowship offers respite care and holidays for disabled people in the UK. Volunteers are needed to help at their five holiday centres for people with physical disabilities to help with the physical care of disabled guests, to socialise with them and join in the holiday. No experience is necessary as staff are always on hand and thorough instructions are always given in advance. Volunteers' ages vary between 16 and 80 – the only requirements are that volunteers must be prepared to work long hours and come with a holiday spirit.

The centres are Sandpipers in Southport, Skylarks in Nottingham, Crabhill House in Surrey, Jubilee Lodge in Essex and Netley Waterside House in Southampton. Winged Fellowship pays travel expenses within the UK and provides board and lodging. Volunteers are required all year round for 1–2 weeks. There are special youth, cricket, horseracing and drama weeks scheduled between regular weeks.

For more information, a brochure or a chat, call Elizabeth on 0171-833 2594 or write to Winged Fellowship, Angel House, 20–32 Pentonville Road, London N1 9XD.

Other organisations that offer voluntary work

Further information on voluntary work in Britain can be obtained from the following organisations.

National Association of Volunteer Bureaux

There are more than 400 volunteer bureaux throughout the UK. Bureaux are 'job shops' for volunteers and provide information about a wide range of local opportunities. They give advice and guidance on how prospective volunteers can use their time and they find people specific jobs by referring them to a statutory agency (for example, a social services department), voluntary organisation or informal volunteer group. Some bureaux also recruit volunteers for projects they have initiated themselves. Check out your local volunteer bureau by looking in the telephone directory under Volunteer Bureaux or Council for Voluntary Service or call into your local Citizens' Advice Bureau or town hall information desk.

For more information, write to National Association of Volunteer Bureaux, St Peter's College, College Road, Saltley, Birmingham B8 3TE (telephone: 0121-327 0265).

The National Youth Agency (NYA)

The NYA publishes an information sheet *Voluntary work and young people* giving details of residential volunteering opportunities in Britain. This is free to young people, £1 to others. The NYA can also provide out details of youth action agencies in England.

For more information, contact The National Youth Agency, 17–23 Albion Street, Leicester LE1 6GD (telephone: 0116 247 1200).

National Youth Council of Ireland

For information on voluntary work in the Republic of Ireland, contact the National Youth Council of Ireland and ask for its *Og Irish Youth Handbook* (free except for postage).

Contact the Information Officer at National Youth Council of Ireland, 3 Montague Street, Dublin 2 (telephone: 00 353 1 478 4122, fax: 00 353 1 478 3974).

The Scottish Community Education Council

The Council promotes community involvement and service by young people in Scotland. It provides an information and advisory service and refers volunteers to appropriate organisations and schemes. It issues information sheets, newsletters, directories of summer opportunities and pamphlets on helping with children, the elderly and the disabled and on other aspects of voluntary work in Scotland.

For more information, contact The Scottish Community Education Council, Rosebery House, 9 Haymarket Terrace, Edinburgh EH12 5EZ (telephone: 0131-313 2488, fax: 0131-313 6800).

Volunteer Centre UK

Based in London, Volunteer Centre UK has a database of voluntary opportunities UK-wide. It can send you a print-out of the voluntary organisations in your area which you may want to contact.

For more information, contact Volunteer Centre UK, 183 Eversholt Street, London NW1 1BU (telephone: 0171-388 9888).

Voluntary Service Belfast (VSB)

VSB is the volunteer bureau for the city of Belfast and arranges voluntary work opportunities on its own project and with other agencies. This involves work with the elderly, disabled, children and young people. The work includes conservation, decorating, visiting, clerical and crime prevention. Applicants must be over 16 and recruitment is throughout the year.

For more information, contact the Director, Voluntary Service Belfast, 70–72 Lisburn Road, Belfast BT9 6AF (telephone: 01232 329499).

Wales Council for Voluntary Action (WCVA)

WCVA provides information about voluntary work opportunities in Wales. Contact WCVA for a copy of *A short guide to voluntary work opportunities in Wales* (WCVA information sheet no. 3) which contains information about voluntary organisations throughout Wales, including addresses and contact names.

For more information, contact Information Department, Wales Council for Voluntary Action, Lys Ifor, Crescent Road, Caerphilly, Mid Glamorgan CF8 1XL (telephone: 01222 869224).

9 Conservation and Renovation Work

There are many organisations offering people the opportunity to gain conservation experience on a working holiday. There is a limited number of opportunities for longer-term work. The work can involve conservation of the countryside or historic buildings; archaeological excavation; protecting birds; clearing litter from beaches; managing woodlands and parks; practical work, such as dry-stone walling; maintenance, or conservation, of buildings, railways and waterways; expedition research and working as a voluntary warden.

Holidays and projects usually last from two days to three weeks, sometimes longer. Experience is not required for most working holidays as training is given, but may be required for longer-term projects. People taking part need to be physically fit and healthy.

The minimum age set is usually 16, but can be 17 or 18. There are often no upper age limits, although some organisations set a maximum age of 25 or 30. Workers usually pay a contribution of between £15–£65 a week towards food and accommodation, on average about £30. However, the contribution required by Earthwatch is considerably higher than this. Travel expenses are not usually paid by the organisation and the accommodation available is usually in hostels, village halls, schools, tents or caravans. See below for details of organisations offering opportunities.

Acorn Projects and Working Holidays (The National Trust)

Acorn Projects runs a series of more than 450 voluntary working holidays in England, Wales and Northern Ireland throughout the year. The work usually consists of outdoor conservation schemes on the Trust's many beautiful properties, often in remote places. The work is hard, but very rewarding. Accommodation is generally in the Trust's own volunteer hostels, called base camps.

Working Holidays can be from two to seven days and there are usually about 12 people per group. Volunteers pay from £15 a week towards the cost of food and accommodation. The minimum age to apply is 17. Approximately 3,500 people are recruited annually. There is no closing date for applications but since women tend to apply earlier the places for women get filled very quickly.

For more information, contact Working Holidays, PO Box 538, Melksham, Wiltshire SN12 8SU (telephone: 01225 790290).

Council for British Archaeology

Information about excavations, and other archaeological fieldwork, can be obtained from the Council for British Archaeology. Individual membership of the Council costs £18 within the UK and includes a magazine, *British Archaeological News*, published ten times a year (on the first Friday of each month with the exception of January and August) with bi-monthly supplements giving details of many projects throughout Britain. Members also automatically belong to CBA Regional Groups which can provide more detailed information on projects in their area. It is possible to subscribe to the magazine without joining the Council for £17 a year. It is then necessary to write to the director of the project(s) which interest(s) you. Some form of subsistence pay is sometimes provided; previous experience is not necessarily required.

For more information, contact the Council for British Archaeology, Bowes Morrell House, 111 Walmgate, York Y01 2UA (telephone: 01904 671417).

Beach Head NT

Volunteers are needed to help clear litter from Cornish beaches. Each morning volunteers are taken to a beach, where they spend up to three hours collecting litter from among rocks and sand dunes. The 12-day 'holidays' (afternoons are free) in July and August cost £125. This covers all meals and accommodation at Beach Head National Trust base camp, a converted barn on a remote part of the coast. Facilities include hot showers, drying room, common room with log fire and fully equipped kitchen. A minibus is available for outings and expeditions. Volunteers help with cleaning, preparing meals and washing-up. Participants pay their own travel expenses and should take a sleeping bag. Enclose a large SAE when writing for further details.

The NT in Cornwall also takes on long-term volunteers. Students should have either relevant qualifications or some practical experience. Accommodation is provided.

For more information, contact Beach Head NT, The Regional Office, Lanhydrock, Bodmin, Cornwall PL30 4ED (telephone: 01208 74281).

The British Trust for Conservation Volunteers (BTCV)
BTCV is the UK's largest practical conservation charity supporting the activities of over 84,000 volunteers in positive steps to improve the environment. Over 600 Natural Break and International Conservation Working Holidays take place every day of the year throughout England, Wales and Northern Ireland and in countries as far afield as the USA and Japan. Prices start from £28 per week including food and accommodation. The accommodation can vary to suit everyone's needs and pocket from a village hall to a fully-catered youth hostel.

Projects range from managing woodlands for wildlife, improving access to the countryside and reviving traditional skills such as dry-stone walling and coppicing. Volunteers must be 16 and over (upper age limit 75). No experience is required. You do, however, need to be physically fit and have plenty of enthusiasm.

BTCV's network of over 90 offices relies on the help of volunteers giving up at least three months of their time. Volunteers receive full training and support in organising and setting up environmental projects, fundraising, publicity and administration of BTCV offices. Voluntary work with BTCV is an excellent stepping stone to a career in conservation.

BTCV also has over 1,400 local groups working most weekends and numerous mid-week projects throughout the country. In addition, BTCV organises over 500 training courses every year covering basic conservation skills to project management, leadership and photography.

For a free Natural Break brochure, contact BTCV's brochure hotline on 01491 824602. For other information, contact the Information Officer, BTCV, 36 St Mary's Street, Wallingford, Oxforshire OX10 0EU (telephone: 01491 839766). For information on BTCV's international conservation projects, see the relevant section in chapter 18.

Cathedral Camps

Volunteers aged 16–30 are needed from the last week in July to the first week in September to work at 26 cathedrals helping with conservation, restoration and maintenance. Each camp lasts one week and costs £33.

For more information, contact the Booking Secretary, Cathedral Camps, 16 Glebe Avenue, Flitwick, Bedfordshire MK45 1HS (telephone: 01525 716237).

Derbyshire International Youth Camp

The Derbyshire International Youth Camp undertakes conservation projects, which recently included the construction of woodland walks and dry-stone walls. Community projects take place around the Derbyshire area, working on children's summer playschemes or projects based in local youth centres.

There are usually 50 young people taking part in the camp each week, half of whom have come from abroad. Accommodation is provided in a residential school; volunteers pay £50 per week to cover food and lodging. A varied leisure programme is arranged including swimming, art, sports, canoeing, climbing, discos, etc. Working with the Youth Camp qualifies under the Duke of Edinburgh's Award Scheme.

The Youth Camp takes place between mid-July and mid-August for four weeks. Applicants should be aged 16–25; overseas applicants are welcome. Application forms are available from the address below and should be returned by 1 May.

For more information, contact Derbyshire International Youth Camp, Derby Youth House, Mill Street, Derby DE1 1DY (telephone: 01332 345538).

Earthwatch

Earthwatch has attracted a great deal of interest. Founded in the USA over 20 years ago, it opened its European office in Oxford four years ago. A non-profit-making organisation, Earthwatch's mission is to match field scientists needing money and manpower with members of the public willing to help. Its services are in great demand since scientific funding is drying up at a time when ecological problems are multiplying.

Earthwatch serves as a bridge between the public and the scientific community. To date, Earthwatch has co-ordinated the involvement of over 40,000 adult men and women in research expeditions worldwide. It has contributed over £17 million and over 4,450,000 hours of labour to earth, human and life sciences in the field. Over 850 science projects, in 104 countries, have been assisted by Earthwatch team members.

Earthwatch team members share the costs of mobilising the research expeditions. For two or three weeks, team members may learn to excavate, map, photograph, gather data, make collections, assist diving operations and share all other field chores associated with professional expedition research. No special skills are required.

Once in the field, volunteers' contributions, which vary with the nature of the project but which currently average £900, cover all the costs, excluding travel. Students and teachers may apply for Earthwatch fellowship grants. Accommodation can range from tents to hotels, and meals are usually local dishes. Earthwatch publishes a bi-monthly magazine containing information on its 160 projects worldwide, which is available with annual membership of £25 (£35 outside Europe).

For more information, contact Earthwatch Europe, Belsyre Court, 57 Woodstock Road, Oxford OX2 6HU (telephone: 01865 516366, fax: 01865 311383).

Ffestinog Railway Company

Volunteers are required to help in the maintenance and running of this famous narrow-gauge railway. A wide variety of work is possible. This can mean working in booking offices, guards' vans, buffet cars, shops, cafés and small sales outlets; cleaning locomotives; working on the footplate and driving; turning, welding, machining, steam-fitting, sheet-metal work, joinery, upholstery and paint work. Other work includes the repair of fences, bridges, culverts and heavy walling. Volunteers also help in maintaining the historic buildings, parks and gardens in which the railway runs. Training is given where necessary. Working for the Ffestinog Railway Company qualifies under the Duke of Edinburgh's Award Scheme. Volunteers should be age 16 and over unless they are in a supervised party. All volunteers must be physically fit. Limited self-catering hostel accommodation is available for regular volunteers, for which a small charge is made. Camping space and lists of local accommodation are also available.

For more information, contact the Volunteer Resource Officer, Ffestinog Railway Company, Harbour Station, Porthmadog, Gwynedd LL49 9NF (telephone: 01766 512340).

The Groundwork Foundation

Formed in 1982, the growing network of Groundwork Trusts works in partnership with business, local authorities and the community. Groundwork is committed to regenerating the built and natural environment across the UK. There are currently 35 local trusts around the country. If you would like to get involved, contact The

Groundwork Foundation, 85–87 Cornwall Street, Birmingham B3 3BY (telephone: 0121-236 8565).

Ironbridge Gorge Museum Trust

The Trust was established in 1967 to conserve, restore and interpret the rich industrial heritage of the Gorge, the birthplace of the Industrial Revolution. The Museum comprises six main sites and has been created around a unique series of industrial monuments, concentrated on the iron and pottery industries, and spreads over some six square miles. Volunteers are needed to work on various sites, doing work that involves industrial archaeology, research, excavation, interpretation of exhibits and general site duties. Accommodation is available on site, or in a youth hostel nearby. Participants pay for their own food. Participants can enter Museum sites free.

For more information, contact Ironbridge Gorge Museum Trust, The Wharfage, Ironbridge, Telford, Shropshire TF8 7AW (telephone: 01952 433522).

National Trust

The National Trust was founded to promote the preservation of fine buildings, beautiful landscapes and historic places. Young volunteers are needed to help with the care and preservation of the countryside and historic buildings through indoor and outdoor conservation projects, which would not otherwise be possible. Recent projects have included sand-dune stabilisation, footpath construction and repair and erosion control. Volunteers should be 17 or over and be fit for hard practical work, eight hours a day, six days a week. Volunteers can work for one to two weeks, weekends or short breaks of three days all year round. An experienced leader and/or a Trust Warden Naturalist supervises all practical work and gives instruction in the safe use of tools. One day is free for recreation and exploration of the local area. Insurance, hostel-type accommodation and food are provided, but volunteers help with catering arrangements and other chores. Old clothes, waterproofs, a sleeping bag and boots or wellingtons should be taken to all projects. Working on the projects qualifies under the Duke of Edinburgh's Award Scheme. Participants pay their own travel costs and contribute £37 towards food and accommodation (£15 for weekends). Volunteers completing 40 hours of voluntary work receive free access to NT properties for a year.

For more information, contact Chris Tews, Residential Projects Co-ordinator, National Trust, Volunteers Office, 33 Sheep Street, Cirencester, Gloucestershire GL7 1QW (telephone: 01285 651818).

The National Trust for Scotland can be contacted at 5 Charlotte Square, Edinburgh EH2 4DU (telephone: 0131-226 5922).

Operation Osprey (RSPB)
Volunteer wardens and cooks are required for the Abernethy Forest-Loch Garten Reserve in the ancient Caledonian Forest, Strathspey. Teams of volunteer wardens keep a 24-hour watch from the hide and are expected to maintain a log of the ospreys' activities. They also spend time talking to visitors about the RSPB's work at Loch Garten. Volunteers work on a shift basis, with every third day free, and also help with camp chores. Applicants need to be 18 and over. For 1995, volunteers are needed for one or more weeks between 25 March and 2 September. Volunteers are accommodated in tents and caravans and full board is provided for a nominal charge of £20 per week. Volunteers should take a sleeping bag, warm clothing and walking boots.

For more information, contact The Royal Society for the Protection of Birds, Grianan, Tulloch, Nethy Bridge, Inverness-shire PH25 3EF (telephone: 01479 831694).

Peak Park Conservation Volunteers
Volunteer opportunities exist for dry-stone walling, scrub and pond clearance, hedge-laying, footpath construction, fencing and other practical countryside work. Volunteers range from 14–65 and groups are on site every weekend

throughout the year. There are limited mid-week tasks, but working holidays are available in partnership with BTCV. Tools and insurance are provided, but not food or travel costs. Local hostels and campsites with good facilities are available, but volunteers must make their own arrangements.

For more information, contact Peak District National Park, National Park Office, Volunteers' Organiser, Aldern House, Baslow Road, Bakewell, Derbyshire DE45 1AE (telephone: 01629 814321).

The Royal Society for the Protection of Birds (RSPB)
The RSPB has places for voluntary wardens on RSPB nature reserves in Britain, assisting the permanent warden, carrying out physical reserve management work, such as clearing ponds or building paths, helping with visitors and carrying out surveys. An interest in, and some knowledge of, birds is an advantage. Accommodation is free but volunteers pay for their own transport to and from the reserve and provide their own food. Volunteers are required all year round. The minimum age of volunteers is 16 and the minimum period to volunteer is one week (Saturday to Saturday). First-time volunteers undergo a one-month trial period.

For more information, contact The Royal Society for the Protection of Birds, Reserves Management Department, The Lodge, Sandy, Bedfordshire SG19 2DL (telephone: 01767 680551).

Scottish Conservation Projects Trust
In Scotland, the independent Scottish Conservation Projects Trust runs weekly and fortnightly Action Breaks from March to December costing £4 a day. SCP's Action Breaks are set up along the same lines as the Natural Breaks run by the British Trust for Conservation Volunteers south of the border, though in somewhat more remote locations, and some include building work.

For more information, contact Scottish Conservation

Projects Trust, Balallan House, 24 Allen Park, Stirling FK8 2QG (telephone: 01786 479697).

Toc H

Toc H organises conservation projects. For more information, see entry in chapter 8.

The Waterway Recovery Group

The Waterway Recovery Group is the national co-ordinating body for voluntary labour on the inland waterways of Britain. It was formed in 1970 to promote and co-ordinate local trusts and societies involved in restoring abandoned and derelict waterways to a navigable state. Volunteers are needed on summer camps to help with this work. There are many active projects including excavating and laying foundations for a new canal bridge, building walls and parapets, dredging and banking, clearing vegetation, pile-driving, fitting lock gates, bricklaying and demolition work.

Volunteers must be 17 and over; parental consent is required for those under 18. The work is unpaid and sometimes unskilled. Volunteers should be fit, willing to work hard in all weathers and able to live harmoniously in fairly close contact with the other 10–20 volunteers at each camp. Volunteers work for one week or more during June–October, Christmas, February and Easter. Basic accommodation is provided in village halls, or similar, plus three good meals a day at a charge of approximately £28 per week. Volunteers should take their own sleeping bag and old clothes, and be prepared to help with domestic chores. Insurance is provided. This work qualifies under the Duke of Edinburgh's Award Scheme. Apply anytime enclosing an SAE. There are, however, limited places.

For more information, contact Neil Edwards, The Waterway Recovery Group, 114 Regent's Park Road, London NW1 8UQ (telephone: 0171-586 2510).

10 Study in the UK

You may want to spend your time out in the UK gaining skills and knowledge that will help you find employment later on. You could consider an administration, computing, language, secretarial or TEFL course. Qualifications in all of these areas will be attractive to employers. These skills may also enable you to gain money from temporary work at any time in your life. Alternatively, you may want to take up a hobby or interest which you have not been able to develop before.

Computer skills

If you take an information technology, computing or administration course you will learn how to word process and to use spreadsheets and databases. Many employers require staff in administrative, clerical or secretarial jobs to be familiar with word processing packages such as WordPerfect or Word. It is also useful to be able to understand spreadsheet packages such as Excel or Lotus 123; you can put this knowledge to some personal use by keeping a record of your finances on a spreadsheet! With computing skills, you will be in a good position to find temporary office work during your time out, and these skills will come in useful during your higher education course and throughout your life. Quite a number of companies no longer employ secretaries, and staff at all levels do their own administration work. Local further education and private colleges run full-time, part-time, intensive courses and evening classes in these subjects. Look in your local reference library for further details or contact your local college direct.

Teaching English as a foreign language (TEFL)

Teaching English as a foreign language is an excellent way to travel, see new countries and to meet people from different cultures. Language schools recruit temporary teachers in the summer and there are opportunities to teach in Europe, South America and Asia. You can get some jobs without a TEFL qualification but this is becoming more difficult and the pay and work conditions are generally worse than for those jobs requiring a qualification. There are a number of TEFL qualifications you could consider taking ranging from the Pilgrims one-week introductory course to the RSA Preparatory Certificate or the Trinity College TESOL qualification.

RSA Preparatory Certificate

Perhaps the most commonly asked-for qualification, the RSA Preparatory Certificate often requires a four-week intensive course but can also be taken on a part-time basis over a longer period. Many schools offering this course mainly recruit graduates. RSA TEFL courses are run at private schools, such as International House in London and the Bell School in Cambridge, and at some colleges of further education.

For more information on where courses are based, contact University of Cambridge Local Examinations Syndicate (UCLES), Syndicate Buildings, 1 Hills Road, Cambridge CB1 2EU (telephone: 01223 553311). The RSA Preparatory Certificate four-week intensive course usually costs between £800–£1,000, so get saving!

Trinity College TESOL (Teaching English to speakers of other languages) qualification

This is taught at private and state institutions. For more information and a list of institutions where this course is taught, contact Trinity College, 16 Park Crescent, London W1N 4AH (telephone: 0171-323 2328).

There are also a number of private organisations that teach their own TEFL course and, in some cases, find applicants jobs abroad. These include Berlitz, Inlingua, Linguarama and Pilgrims. Their addresses are listed below.

Berlitz
9–13 Grosvenor Street
London W1A 3BZ

Inlingua
Rodney Lodge
Rodney Road
Cheltenham
Gloucestershire GL50 1JF
Telephone: 01242 253171

Linguarama
New Oxford House
16 Waterloo Street
Birmingham
West Midlands B2 6UG
Telephone: 0121-632 5925

Pilgrims
8 Vernon Place
Canterbury
Kent CT1 3HG
Telephone: 01227 762111

Learning another language

You may also want to consider improving those spoken language skills if you intend to travel abroad later on in the year, or work for an international organisation after higher education. The cheaper option is to take up an evening course at a local college of further education. The other, more expensive, alternative is to take a course at a private school such as the Institut Français or Goethe Institut in London. In private schools, classes tend to be smaller and thus you can get more individual attention.

Organisations you may want to contact regarding language courses in the UK are listed below.

Alliance Française
1 Dorset Square
London NW1 6PY
Telephone: 0171-723 6439

Alliance Française runs French courses in London and France.

Goethe Institut
50 Prince's Gate
Exhibition Road
London SW7 2PH
Telephone: 0171-411 3436/3451

The Goethe Institut offers German summer courses for children (10–13) and teenagers (13–15 and 14–17). These programmes are run at boarding schools in Germany and combine intensive German language instruction with a varied activities programme including sports and crafts. The Institut can also provide information to adults on language courses.

Institut Français
14 Cromwell Place
South Kensington
London SW7 2JR
Telephone: 0171-581 2701

The Institut Français runs French courses in London.

International House
106 Piccadilly
London W1V 9FL
Telephone: 0171-499 6593/491 2598

International House runs language courses in London and at affiliated schools abroad.

Evening classes

Alternatively, if you are working, you may want to take up an evening course for pleasure and, in this case, you will have many courses to choose from at your local college of further education. Ideas for courses include art and design, pottery, car maintenance, drama, dance, aromatherapy, photography and there are many more... If you are over 19, it is likely that you will have to pay the full fees for most courses, unless you are unemployed in which case you will qualify for reduced fees. If you are under 19, and taking a full-time course, you should not have to pay course fees. You will be able to find details about the courses available in your area from your careers service, local reference library and from individual college prospectuses. Enrolment for part-time courses is usually at the beginning of September but enquire earlier in the year because some courses get filled up quickly.

Sports instructors' qualifications

You could spend some time taking a sport instructor's qualification during your time out. You will then be in a much better position to apply for sports instructor jobs on children's summer camps and at activity centres.

For more information on courses, and where you can do them, contact the Sports Council, Information Centre, 16 Upper Woburn Place, London WC1H 0QP (telephone: 0171-388 1277). The Sports Council publishes *Governing Bodies of Sport Address Book.*

The Sail Training Association (STA) Schooners

STA Schooners runs adventure training courses all year round for people aged 16–69 on the sail training schooners *Sir Winston Churchill* and *Malcolm Miller.* Sailing is generally in Britain but in the winter takes place around the Canary Islands. A voyage is fun, hard work and exciting.

The ships need full crews of 55 to sail them and everyone on board forms a vital part of the team to hoist sails, set them to catch the wind, tack or gybe the ship, stow the sails when they are finished with, take the helm, keep a look out and many other activities. The work can be hard at times; and weather conditions can be cold, wet and stormy. No special skills or experience are required.

Prices start from £180 for three days' sailing around Oban and go up to about £806 for a 12 days' Tall Ships Race to Amsterdam. For 12–13 days' sailing around Britain, prices vary between £576–£888. The voyages can cost more than some young people can afford. The STA, and its volunteer branches all over the country, raise money for grants towards voyage fees which can be made available to people depending on their circumstances.

For more information, contact STA Schooners, 2a The Hard, Portsmouth, Hampshire PO1 3PT (telephone: 01705 832055).

3

Taking Time Out in Continental Europe

11 Paid Employment in Continental Europe

There is a variety of opportunities open to those who want to take time out and work, study or travel in another part of Europe. To get the most out of many of these options, you will need a good grasp of the language of your destination country.

Insurance

Whatever you decide to do – work, study or travel – it is sensible to arrange insurance cover for accidents, sickness and loss of baggage and possessions. Some workcamps and voluntary agencies arrange insurance cover for people taking part in their projects but this is not always the case. ISIS (International Student Insurance Service) provides reasonably priced insurance cover for young people spending time abroad. Details of ISIS are available from Endsleigh Insurance Services Ltd, Endsleigh House, Ambrose Street, Cheltenham, Gloucestershire GL50 3NR.

Residents in the UK are entitled to reciprocal medical treatment in European Union countries, ie you get the same level of treatment for the same fee as a citizen of the country you are visiting. The certificate that entitles you to reciprocal healthcare (E111) must be filled in and stamped by the post office before you leave the UK.

The European Union

The UK is now very much part of the European Union and, increasingly, people are planning a career with a European dimension in mind. The Single European Market means that businesses can trade freely throughout the 15 European Union states (Austria, Belgium, Denmark, Finland, France, Germany, Greece, Italy, Luxembourg, The Netherlands, Portugal, the Republic of

Ireland, Spain, Sweden and the UK) and with the two EFTA (European Free Trade Association) countries which have signed the EEA (European Economic Area) agreement (Iceland and Norway). Liechtenstein will be joining the EEA soon; Switzerland is still part of EFTA but has decided not to sign the EEA agreement.

British companies are developing partnerships with companies in other parts of Europe and are setting up branches in other member states of the EU. As a result, Europe-wide companies are emerging. When recruiting, these companies are looking for people who have a good grasp of other European languages, who have spent some time doing short-term work abroad and who are not afraid of working abroad and with people of differing cultures.

In the following section, you will find information relating to both short- and long-term work opportunities, including work placements, which are periods of time spent in employment, often during further or higher education or training. The job opportunities include work as an au pair or nanny, work on children's camps, work within the travel and tourism industry, teaching English as a foreign language (TEFL), office work, work as a sales representative and farm work. For all of these opportunities, you will find addresses and contact details of organisations that recruit staff. Many of these organisations are based in the UK, which makes your job search easier. You will find details of organisations that provide general information on employment in the country they represent in the Country Index in Part 5.

Work as an au pair or nanny

Perhaps one of the easiest jobs to find abroad is that of an au pair or nanny. There are a number of agencies, many of which are based in the UK, that recruit nannies and au pairs for other parts of Europe. There are opportunities to work during the summer for one to three months, or for a longer period of 10–12 months. Most positions are open to young people between the ages of 18–30 and require only babysitting experience. However, the more childcare experience you have, the easier you will find the work. But most of all, to be a successful au pair you have to be flexible and willing to adapt to a different way of life.

Some knowledge of the language of the country is sometimes necessary and often au pairs/nannies are given time off to attend language classes, which may be paid for by the host family. Full board and lodging are provided and the average pocket money per week is between £30–£40, but it is possible to earn more than this.

Au pairs/nannies usually work about 30 hours a week over six days and also have some evenings off. They may have to do some light housework in addition to looking after the children and will be asked to babysit in the evening. Home Office guidelines state that au pairs and nannies should not work more than two evenings a week. Some agencies require references and applicants need to be physically fit. A full driving licence will also be needed for some positions.

Below, you will find the details of agencies in the UK and other parts of Europe that recruit nannies and au pairs. It is worth applying to several different agencies so that you have a choice of family and area in the country of your choice.

Aaron Employment Agency

Aaron Employment Agency places au pairs and nannies in Europe for a minimum of six weeks at any time in the year. It also places au pairs in Canada for a minimum of one year. Au pairs can earn approximately £140 a month for a 30-hour week, five days a week. Nannies earn approximately £480 per month for a 37–42-hour week over five days and must have relevant qualifications such as a certificate or diploma awarded by NNEB or BTEC, Norland or Montessori training or live-in experience. For some positions babysitting experience only will be necessary.

Requirements depend on the position offered; more experience will be required if the nanny is in sole charge of the children. Board and accommodation are provided free of charge.

For more information, contact Aaron Employment Agency, Suite C, The Courtyard, Stanley Road, Tunbridge Wells, Kent TN1 2RJ (telephone: 01892 546601, fax: 01892 544827).

Accueil Familial des Jeunes Etrangers

Accueil Familial des Jeunes Etrangers arranges for au pairs aged 18–30 to stay with French families all over France. Applicants must be able to speak some French. Summer placements are arranged from one to three months; long stays until the end of the school year in July start 1–15 September and 1–15 January. The agency also provides accommodation through its paying guest service.

Applications should be made two weeks before the proposed starting date of work to Accueil Familial des Jeunes Etrangers, 23 rue du Cherche-Midi, 75006 Paris, France (telephone: 00 33 1 42 22 50 34).

Atlantis Youth Exchange

Atlantis Youth Exchange is a Norwegian organisation that offers au pair programmes in all western European countries including Norway and in a number of other countries including the USA.

For more information, contact Atlantis Youth Exchange, Rolf Hofmosgate 18, 0655 Oslo, Norway (telephone: 00 47 22 670043, fax: 00 47 22 686808).

Au Pair International

Au Pair International places au pairs in Italy in the summer (June–September) or longer term (6–12 months from September). The work is mostly childminding, with some housework. Pocket money is approximately £30 per week plus full board and lodging. Au pairs work approximately six hours per day with one complete day and two or three evenings free per week. Applicants should be aged 18–30; babysitting experience is an advantage.

For more information, contact Au Pair International sas, via S Stefano, 32–40125 Bologna, Italy (telephone: 00 39 51 26 75 75, fax: 00 39 51 23 65 94).

Au Pairs Italy

Au Pairs Italy places au pairs, mother's helps, nannies and governesses in Italy. During the summer holidays, girls are required for about three months, occasionally even for one to two months. The normal length of stay throughout the year is 6–12 months, with a few shorter vacancies usually available. The minimum age is 18.

Send an SAE for more information to Au Pairs Italy, 46 The Rise, Sevenoaks, Kent TN13 1RJ (telephone: 01732 451522).

Avalon Agency

Avalon arranges au pair placements for 25 hours' work a week in the UK, continental Europe and USA. Au pairs are provided with pocket money, food and accommodation in exchange for light housework and childcare as per international agreements.

For more information, contact Avalon Agency, 53 Station Road, Shalford, Guildford, Surrey GU4 8HA (telephone: 01483 63640).

Childcare International Ltd

This organisation has three separate branches: Childcare Europe, Childcare America and Childcare Canada. See chapter 16 in Part 4 for more details of Childcare America and Childcare Canada.

Childcare Europe

Au pairs, nannies and mother's helps are placed in Austria, Belgium, France, Italy, The Netherlands, Spain and Switzerland. A commitment of 6–12 months is preferred but there are also opportunities for three-month seasonal placements. Ski au pair positions are available during the winter months. Experience with children is useful. The preferred age range is 18–27 years and the amount of pocket money varies with experience. Full back-up is available in the country of placement.

For more information, contact Childcare International Ltd, Trafalgar House, Grenville Place, London NW7 3SA (telephone: 0181-959 3611/906 3116, fax: 0181-906 3461).

Club de Relaciones Culturales Internacionales (RCI)
Club de RCI is a cultural, educational and language association which has extensive international programmes for students and adults from Spain and other countries. People from the UK may be interested in their au pair in Spain programme. This programme places foreign students in families in Spain. Au pairs are asked to help with the children, five hours a day, with languages, babysitting and light housework. In return, they live as a member of the family, with board and lodging provided, and receive a monthly allowance. Club de RCI offers au pairs in Spain beginners, intermediate and advanced level classes in Spanish. It also organises au pair programmes and study abroad programmes for Spanish students.

For more information, contact Club de Relaciones Culturales Internacionales, Ferraz, 82, 28008 Madrid, Spain (telephone: 00 34 1 541 71 03).

Contacts
Contacts arranges au pair placements with French families during the summer and other holidays and for up to 12 months. The minimum age for applicants is 18. An international reply coupon must accompany applications. Contacts also offers linguistic stays in France (Tours, Paris, Biarritz) for young people, arranging accommodation with families and in residences. It also runs lessons for young people who are 12 years and above in classes with a maximum of 15 pupils.

For more information, contact Contacts, 53 rue Nationale, 37000 Tours, France (telephone: 00 33 47 20 20 57).

Experiment in International Living (EIL)

EIL organises au pair stays in Europe, including France, Germany and Spain, plus individual and group homestays and language courses throughout the world and an au pair programme to the USA. See the section on paying guests and exchange visits in chapter 14 for more details.

For more information on the au pair programme, contact the EIL UK branch at Otesaga, West Malvern Road, Malvern, Worcestershire WR14 4EN (telephone: 01684 562577).

Experiment Séjours Educatifs Internationaux

This agency places au pairs, aged 18–25, in French families for periods of 3–18 months. Au pairs work 30 hours a week looking after children and doing light housework and must possess at least an intermediate level of French. Au pairs are provided with their own room and meals and are paid a monthly salary of FF1,600. They pay for their travel to France.

For more information, contact Experiment Séjours Educatifs Internationaux, 89 rue de Turbigo, 75003 Paris, France (telephone: 00 33 1 42 78 50 03).

Galentinas Nannies and Au Pairs

Galentinas provides professional guidance to qualifying candidates seeking one-year positions with carefully screened families in Europe, mostly in Greece, and the USA. Nannies and au pairs are offered excellent conditions and benefits, return air fare, medical insurance, etc. There is no candidate placement fee. The minimum length of service is one year, or 2–3 months during the summer season.

For more information, contact Galentinas Nannies and Au Pairs, PO Box 51181, GR 145.10 Kifissia, Greece (telephone: 00 30 1 808 1005).

Helping Hands Agency

This agency places au pairs/mother's helps throughout Europe and in Canada (as well as in the UK). Applicants should have at least basic childcare experience. Knowledge of the relevant language is highly desirable for overseas placements. Work is for three months during the summer or a minimum of six months at other times of the year. Applicants should be between the ages of 17–27. Pocket money starts at £30–£35 per week for au pairs and increases considerably for mother's helps. Full board is provided. Au pairs work five hours a day, five days a week and do some babysitting (not more than two evenings a week). Mother's helps work full-time; hours are negotiated with the family.

For more information, please send an SAE for a brochure and application form to Helping Hands Agency, 10 Hertford Road, Newbury Park, Ilford, Essex IG2 7HQ (telephone: 01702 602067).

Home from Home

Home from Home places au pairs with families in Austria, Belgium, France, Germany, Italy, The Netherlands, Spain, Switzerland and the UK. The minimum age accepted is 18 and au pairs must be prepared to stay a minimum of six months, except in the summer when they may work for 2–3 months, and at least one year in Switzerland.

For more information, contact Home from Home, Walnut Orchard, Chearsley, Aylesbury, Buckinghamshire HP18 0DA (telephone and fax: 01844 208561).

International Catholic Society for Girls (ACISJF)

The agency organises au pair posts in France and The Netherlands for English girls (who need not be Roman Catholics) over the summer. For periods of 6–10 months, positions are available in France, Germany, The Netherlands and Spain. The minimum age is 18 years and the minimum stays are three months over the summer, ten months from September, six months from January.

For more information, write with an SAE to the International Catholic Society for Girls (ACISJF), St

Patrick's International, 24 Great Chapel Street, London W1V 3AF (telephone: 0171-734 2156/439 0116).

Inter-Séjours

Inter-Séjours places au pairs in Austria, the Canary Islands, France, Germany, Italy and Spain. Duties include housekeeping and looking after children, five hours a day, six days a week, and two or three evenings a week babysitting. Work is for three months during the summer, or 6–12 months at any time throughout the year. Applicants should be aged 18–25 years and have some knowledge of the language of the country they wish to visit. Pocket money is around £150 per month in France and Germany. Paying guests can also stay with families in France (many families within the Loire valley), Germany, Italy and Spain and in the USA. Two or three hours of lessons per day plus sporting activities and excursions can be arranged or guests can just stay with families and not take lessons.

For more information, contact Inter-Séjours, 179 rue de Courcelles, 75017 Paris, France (telephone: 00 33 1 47 630681)

Jolaine Au Pair Agency

This agency provides au pair and mother's help placements throughout the year with families in many parts of Europe for 6–12-month stays. Some positions are available for male applicants and, during the summer months, positions for two- or three-month stays are available. Applicants are responsible for paying their air fare, insurance, school fees, etc. The agency asks for a small fee for arranging the placement; this is currently £40 and is payable on the applicant's acceptance of a suitable position. Once placed, all applicants have the support and use of services provided by Jolaine's agents abroad.

Paying guest stays are also arranged in other parts of Europe, with or without courses, for a minimum period of one week. See chapter 14 for more details.

For more information, write, enclosing a large SAE, to Jolaine Au Pair Agency, 18 Escot Way, Barnet, Hertfordshire EN5 3AN (telephone: 0181-449 1334, fax: 0181-449 9183).

Mondial Au Pair Agency

Mondial arranges au pair posts, for girls only, in Austria, France and Spain for a minimum of six months. Applicants need to complete the registration form and return it with two photographs, two written references, a CV in the form of a personal letter and a medical certificate to show a good state of health. Mondial then tries to find a suitable family who will contact applicants direct. This may take several weeks as families and applicants need to be well matched. An engagement fee of £40 is payable when the offer of a suitable position is accepted. Au pairs can then use the services of agents in Barcelona, Paris, Nice or Vienna if they have any problems.

For more information, contact Mondial Au Pair Agency, 32 Links Road, West Wickham, Kent BR4 0QW (telephone: 0181-777 6271/0510)

ÖKISTA (Austrian Committee for International Educational Exchange)

ÖKISTA places au pairs with Austrian families in Vienna, main cities and country areas. Au pairs are expected to help with children and do light housework, five/six hours daily, plus babysitting two/three evenings per week by arrangement. They receive one day off per week and time to attend German language classes. Board and lodging are provided with pocket money of £150 per month.

Stays are for 6–12 months throughout the year but language classes are not available during the summer as courses start in September, January and at Easter. Two- to three-month stays, without language classes, are available during the summer. The agency offers au pair programmes including travel in Austria, sightseeing and meetings with other au pairs. Reduced air fares, train tickets and medical insurance are available.

ÖKISTA also provides home stays with Austrian families as paying guests and runs German classes in Vienna for students, adults and au pairs throughout the year.

For more information, contact Austrian Committee for International Educational Exchange (ÖKISTA), Garnisongasse 7, 1090 Vienna Austria (telephone: 00 431 401 48 225 or 226).

Pro Filia

Pro Filia places au pairs with families in the regions of France bordering Switzerland and Geneva for stays of 12 months or more.

For more information, contact Pro Filia, 51 Rue de Carouge, 1205 Geneva, Switzerland (telephone and fax: 00 41 22/329 84 62 Tuesday/Wednesday/Thursday 8.30am to 5.00pm).

Séjours Internationaux Linguistiques et Culturels

This organisation places au pairs with families in France for a minimum of eight weeks in the summer, or for six months or more (preferably a school year) starting in September.

Enquiries should be made to SILC, c/o Christiane Burt, Euro-Pair Agency, 28 Derwent Avenue, Pinner, Middlesex HA5 4QJ (telephone: 0181-421 2100, fax: 0181-428 6416). Enquiries can also be made to Séjours Internationaux, 32 Rempart de l'Est, 16022 Angoulême, Cedex, France (telephone: 00 33 45 97 41 10).

South-Eastern Au Pair Bureau

Placements are available in Austria, Belgium, Denmark, Finland, France, Germany, Italy, The Netherlands, Norway, Spain, Sweden and Switzerland and there is a network of associates in these countries to assist with placing suitable au pairs. Information is also available on au pair work in America; these placings are for one year.

In Europe, vacancies are available in cities, towns, villages, coastal and country areas. There is rarely a problem finding a suitable family for an au pair wishing to stay a minimum of six months. Au pairs live as part of a family and are provided with full board and lodging and pocket money of around £35 per week. Working hours are 30 per week and sufficient free time is available for language classes and pursing personal interests. In some countries, other opportunities are available to increase the number of hours worked and pocket money is paid accordingly. This includes nanny work where suitable wages are offered in accordance with age and experience.

For more information, contact South-Eastern Au Pair Bureau, 39 Rutland Avenue, Thorpe Bay, Essex SS1 2XJ (telephone: 01702 601911).

Students Abroad Limited

This organisation, established in 1976, specialises in placing young people as au pairs. Working with their comprehensive network of agents, they match applicants with host families throughout the European Union, Turkey and the USA.

Au pairs live as part of a family, helping with childcare and light housework. A room and full board are provided. Some childcare/babysitting experience is preferred. Basic language skills are preferred but not essential. As it is not always easy to adjust to living with a family in a different culture, applicants are advised to make sure this is what they want before making a commitment.

Posts in Europe are for a minimum of six months although some two-month summer placements are possible in France, Italy and Spain. Demand for summer posts is high so early application is essential. The weekly pay is £35–£40 for approximately 30 hours' work. Free time is given for language classes (not available during summer). Minimum age is 18; maximum age is 27.

All applicants are required to complete a registration form, which should be returned with eight photographs, two references, a clean medical certificate and an introduction letter to the prospective host family.

A £40 service fee is required. This is refunded in full in

the unlikely event that the applicant does not accept a post. An information pack is also available at the cost of £6. This includes an introduction to the host country, helpful hints on discount travel, work permit/visa requirements, comprehensive health/travel insurance (including free telephone or postal insurance brokerage service), E111 and a health information booklet.

Requirements vary for those who want to work in the USA. See chapter 16 in Part 4 for more details.

For information and a registration form, please send a large SAE to Students Abroad Ltd, 11 Milton View, Hitchin, Hertfordshire SG4 0QD (telephone: 01462 438909).

Universal Care

Universal Care specialises in providing opportunities for young people to become au pairs in western European countries. They have associated agents in France, Germany, Italy and Spain who select suitable families for prospective au pairs. Provided that the young person wishes to be placed for at least six months, there is no difficulty in finding a suitable family. Prospective au pairs should write to Universal Care and will be sent full details of the service together with an application form. This needs to be completed and returned with four passport photos, a medical clearance form from their doctor, two references and a letter to the prospective family. They will then be given full details of a family that is interested in them and can choose to accept the position or not. Only when they have accepted a position are they required to pay the agency fee of £40 plus VAT.

Universal Care's office is open during normal office hours and has a 24-hour answering machine. It is licensed by the Department of Employment and is a member of the Federation of Recruitment and Employment Services.

For more information and an application form, contact Universal Care Ltd, Chester House, 9 Windsor End, Beaconsfield, Buckinghamshire HP9 2JJ (telephone: 01494 678811).

Verein für Internationale Jugendarbeit

This is a Christian Women's Association that is affiliated to the YWCA with headquarters in Germany. It places young women and men of 18 to 24 as au pairs with German families for stays of between six months to two years. It also places German au pairs abroad. Au pairs receive £120–£135 pocket money per month. A reasonable knowledge of German is essential. Au pairs are offered help and advice and, in many cities, this organisation runs international youth clubs.

For more information, contact Verein für Internationale Jugendarbeit, 39 Craven Road, London W2 3BX (telephone: 0171-723 0216).

Working with children on holiday camps

A number of travel companies employ young people as couriers to escort under-18s to Europe for a variety of holidays, which range from educational tours to activity and adventure-type holidays. On the latter, you would be expected to participate in many of the activities offered, such as canoeing, windsurfing and sailing. There are also opportunities for young people to look after, entertain and arrange activities for children on summer camps.

PGL Young Adventure Ltd

PGL Young Adventure Ltd recruits staff to work at residential activity centres both in the UK and France. There are vacancies for outdoor activity instructors, for group leaders (responsible for the organisation and welfare of children) and for various support roles. The latter include kitchen staff, drivers, nurses, maintenance and domestic staff. Please see the PGL section in chapter 7 for more detailed information.

For information on PGL opportunities, contact Personnel Department, 839 Alton Court, Penyard Lane, Ross-on Wye, Hereford and Worcester HR9 5NR (telephone: 01989 767833).

Eurocamp plc

Eurocamp plc employs over 1,500 overseas staff every summer to work on campsites in 12 European countries. Staff are expected to provide excellent customer service at all times to holidaymakers who stay in tents or mobile homes where everything is provided. There is a variety of positions available including courier, children's courier, activity organiser, cleaning and maintenance courier and montage/demontage assistants. Montage assistants are needed early in the season to put up the tents and get the equipment ready; demontage assistants work late in the season taking down the tents and putting the equipment into store. Applicants do not need languages for these two positions; they just need to be physically strong. Other positions require different skills and abilities. However, most require a good working knowledge of one other major European language, applicants who are aged 18 or over and who are available from April/May to September/October. Interviews are conducted around the UK.

To apply, contact Eurocamp Summer Jobs (Ref YO), PO Box 170, Liverpool L70 1ES or the Overseas Recruitment Department, Knutsford (telephone: 01565 625522). Telephone applications are preferred.

Canvas Holidays Ltd

Canvas Holidays Ltd recruits people who are 18 or over, who are available from April to October, who have a working knowledge of a foreign language and who are hard-working, friendly and flexible. Jobs available include those for campsite courier (putting up and taking down tents and looking after holidaymakers), children's courier, watersports courier and activity courier. Most of the positions are based in France but there are also some vacancies in Austria, Germany, Italy, Luxembourg, Spain and Switzerland. Experience of dealing with the public would be useful for most positions. Pay is £85 per week and accommodation is provided.

Write in for an application form to the Overseas Personnel Manager at Canvas Holidays Ltd, 12 Abbey Park Place, Dunfermline, Fife KY12 7PD (telephone: 01383 644018).

Working in the tourist industry

Many holiday companies employ people as couriers, tour guides, ski representatives and hotel/chalet staff during the summer/winter seasons. Knowledge of a foreign language is often essential and applicants usually need to be at least 18. Some companies prefer people over 21.

Working as a courier or overseas representative

Tour operators usually employ staff as couriers or overseas representatives to assist their clients while they are on holiday. Couriers generally travel with the party from the start and stay with the same group for the duration of the trip. Overseas representatives are usually permanently stationed in the summer or winter resort to welcome and look after the clients when they arrive. People usually work in these positions for a season or two and then move on to another career. Tour operators are usually looking for people with a good general education and proven proficiency in a language (be warned: your ability may be tested in the interview!). Most tour operators recruit people over 18 or 20 years and look for evidence of maturity and experience of dealing with the public. Competition for jobs is fierce.

For details of tour operators, or indeed any organisations connected with the travel industry in the UK such as travel agents, airlines, hotels, national tourist offices, car, coach and sea travel specialists, look in the *Travel Trade Gazette Directory* which should be available in large reference libraries. There are also North America, Asia Pacific and Europe guides listing overseas travel agents and tour operators, cruise line companies, hotels, airports, airlines and details of organisations dealing with sea and land travel.

You can order your own copy of the *Travel Trade Gazette Directory*, which, like the other guides, is fairly expensive at £65 but very comprehensive, from TTG Directories, Riverbank House, Angel Lane, Tonbridge, Kent TN9 1SE (telephone: 01732 362666).

Christina Hunter

Overseas representative Thomsons Holidays case-study

Christina is currently studying for an MSc in Tourism Management at Surrey University. Her long-term aim is to progress into management in the tourism and hospitality industry.

‘Last year, after graduating with a degree in Spanish and Portuguese, I travelled around Australia, the Far East and Brazil for six months and then worked for six months as a representative for Thomsons Holidays in Greece. Before working for Thomsons, I also managed to fit in a month working as an interpreter/chaperone for the Miss World competition.

I applied to Thomsons because I felt that working as a representative would give me excellent practical experience that would help me enter the tourism and hospitality industry later.

The selection procedure was fairly gruelling. My language skills were tested and I also had to prepare a presentation in which I was selling an excursion. After that, I had an individual interview, a group interview and I had to do some written tests (which tested logic) and take part in a group discussion. I managed to stay the course and was offered a job. I was then sent on a week's training course which covered problem-solving, dealing with clients, giving presentations and guiding. The group had to take part in role-plays where group members had to deal with awkward customers. The training course prepares you well for the work ahead. I hadn't realised how much client contact working as a representative involves.

A week before I was to leave, I was told that I was being sent to Rhodes. I had a week to prepare myself before the holidaymakers arrived. I spent time getting to know the area, collecting information about the island, going on all the excursions and putting together my welcome meeting. When the first guests arrived, I felt pretty nervous and I found the first welcome meeting a nightmare. It's difficult to be nice to people all the time! You have to be tolerant, assertive and calm.

During the season, my job involved liaising with hotels, organising and selling excursions, dealing with clients' problems and administrative work. Every day presented a new challenge, and a new problem! The general public can be awkward and arrangements don't always go to plan; I spent one night trying to get rooms for 19 people when there were no rooms available anywhere. You have to be diplomatic and be able to get on with all types of people.

I had a great time in Rhodes and met many different people. I had lots of free time and had a full social life. I found the people in Rhodes very friendly and I enjoyed being immersed in the Greek culture and language. I did not, however, know any Greek before I went and it wasn't needed most of the time.

I feel that I gained some excellent experience in Rhodes and developed some useful skills such as working in a team, time management, how to handle the public and giving presentations. Working as a representative boosted my confidence and I learnt how to handle a situation where people were relying on me.

I feel that my break from study was very valuable. I am now concentrating my efforts on trying to get into the tourism and hospitality industry in a permanent position. ’

The address of Thomsons Holidays is Greater London House, Hampstead Road, London NW1 7SD (telephone: 0171-387 9321).

Working in ski resorts

There is a variety of jobs available in ski resorts ranging from positions for chalet staff, bar staff and cleaning staff to ski guide (a certificate in skiing is usually required) and overseas representative. It is essential to apply early for these positions – usually during the summer and before the end of September. You will find details of one organisation offering ski resort opportunities below. For more information and contacts, see Part 5.

Jobs in the Alps

Jobs in the Alps is an agency which places British workers in mountain resorts in Austria and Switzerland for the winter and summer seasons. Applicants for jobs come from a variety of backgrounds; some have worked in hotels, offices, factories, etc and others apply before, during and after university. Most applicants have some knowledge of French or German.

The positions for which there are vacancies include waiting staff, buffet staff, kitchen staff, hall porters and night porters, chamberpeople, receptionists, bar staff, cashiers and cleaners in hotels, restaurants, mountain restaurants and cafés and occasional au pair work in families.

Most winter jobs start early to mid-December and last until mid-April; there are a few in January when replacements may be needed. Most summer jobs are for three months, from mid/end June to mid/end September. Some are from Easter to October, very few are just July and August. Workers are on probation for two weeks and then, if the employer is satisfied, they can carry on but must commit themselves to the whole season.

All employees have free board and lodging. They are entitled to cheap lift passes and cheap travel. Employees work about 45 hours a week, usually with two free days. The pay ranges between £120–£150 (less for au pair work) a week depending on the job.

Jobs in the Alps does not send workers to France and

Germany as the state employment bureaux have a monopoly. However, the ALPOTELS aptitude tests used by Jobs in the Alps are accepted by French and German employers who wish to recruit British workers.

Applicants must be at least 18 and work experience will be required for some positions. For some jobs language skills are essential; for others, such as backroom jobs, this will be less important. Approximately 200 people are sent to jobs for the winter season and 150 for the summer. Early application for all positions is highly recommended (by the end of September for winter positions and the end of April for summer positions) as Jobs in the Alps receives approximately 10,000 enquiries from interested applicants each year.

For more information, contact Jobs in the Alps, PO Box 388, London SW1X 8LX (telephone: 0171-235 8205).

Working in hotels

There are opportunities, if you have language skills, to work in hotels and restaurants throughout Europe.

Horizon HPL

Horizon HPL arranges placements for Europeans in hotels, restaurants and companies in France and the UK. The primary aim of the placements is for people to improve their language skills, while at the same time gaining valuable work experience. Obviously, trainees rapidly improve their language skills in the workplace. In addition, they can also follow a language training course provided by Horizon. This language training can last two or four months and consists of one three-hour class per week, in groups of a maximum of five people. It complements the language that trainees pick up at work.

People of any age can apply to Horizon HPL although the majority are 17–30. For the placements in France, applicants are invited to interview and undergo a French test. Formal qualifications in French are not required but, at the minimum, a basic knowledge of the language is required.

Placements in hotels and restaurants include those for general assistant, commi (assistant) chef, chef, waiter/waitress, bar and reception work. Placements can last from two months to a year. When placing applicants, Horizon HPL bears in mind the level of language applicants possess. Previous work experience is not required for most positions. Those placed in hotels and restaurants are given free accommodation and receive pocket money of approximately £40 a week.

Horizon charges a fee of £240 for hotel and restaurant placements. If applicants decide to take up the language training, they pay an extra £160 for two months' tuition and £300 for four months' tuition. People can also go to France and just undergo the language training which costs £180 for 18 hours in one month.

Lara Manning

Horizon HPL case-study

Lara is currently at university studying French and Italian. She took a year out to improve her French and worked in a hotel in Paris.

'I applied for a degree in French and German for entry in October 1993 and then I decided to take a break from study and arranged to defer my place for a year. I worked in a library for a few months but my main aim was to spend some time abroad improving my spoken French. I applied to lots of organisations, many of which did not reply, and then I came across Horizon HPL. I applied to them in January 1994 and, within a month, I was working as a receptionist in a Paris hotel which was ten minutes' away from the Eiffel Tower. I worked a 35-hour week, mostly at the weekend, and had two full days off a week. My accommodation was free, and was arranged for me, and the hotel paid me FF1,770 (approximately £221) a month plus half the cost of my orange card (monthly metro card) each month.

The hotel was family-run with 32 rooms and my work

involved taking reservations, confirmations, liaising with room staff and answering general questions about what to do in Paris, how to get to places, etc. I made a few mistakes in the first month but the hotel management was very supportive and understanding. The first few weeks were very challenging, speaking French all the time, but I soon fitted in and my French improved dramatically. I had decided to pay for a weekly three-hour French lesson run by Horizon HPL and here I met, and made friends with, other trainees on placement with Horizon.

I had originally intended to stay in France for three months but, since I was enjoying myself, I decided to stay on. Fortunately, one of the staff at the hotel where I was placed was going away for a while and so I was kept on for an extra two months.

I would definitely recommend a similar experience to other people. It's an excellent way of gaining useful work experience, learning a language and seeing a different way of life. I found the hotel and Horizon supportive and met a lot of new people. Quite a lot of people who are placed in France by Horizon go on to find permanent employment with other companies.

I am now studying French and Italian at university, rather than French and German. My experience in France encouraged me to take up a new language from scratch. ’

For more information, contact Horizon HPL's London office at Southbank House, Black Prince Road, London SE1 7SJ (telephone: 0171-735 8171) or the Paris office at 17 rue Pache, 75011 Paris, France (telephone: 00 33 1 40 24 09 31).

Teaching English as a foreign language (TEFL)

There are many opportunities to teach English in Europe. It is often necessary to have a degree (but not necessarily in English); a recognised TEFL certificate will increase your chances of employment and enable you to secure a higher salary. There are two main TEFL qualifications that are worth acquiring. These are the RSA Preparatory Certificate and Trinity College's TESOL qualification. For more details, see chapter 10 in Part 2.

TEFL jobs are usually advertised in the education section of the *Guardian* on Tuesdays, the *Times Educational Supplement* on Fridays and *EFL Gazette* (contact the Subscriptions Department, 106 Dunyeats Road, Broadstone, Dorset BH18 8AN). Some schools running TEFL courses (eg International House in London and the Bell School in Cambridge) are also notified of TEFL jobs abroad.

Jobs in western Europe are not easy to acquire. There is, however, an increasing number of TEFL jobs in eastern Europe (Czech Republic, Hungary, Poland, Romania and Slovak Republic), the Baltic states (Estonia, Latvia and Lithuania), the states of the former Soviet Union, the Far East (Indonesia, Korea, Taiwan, Thailand and Vietnam) and South America.

The British Council has a number of schools overseas and recruits from London and locally. Often it looks for people with TEFL experience. The address of the British Council is OAS, Medlock Street, Manchester M15 4AA. International House in London also recruits for a number of its schools abroad. Its Teacher Selection Service is based at 45 Hertford Street, London W1Y 7TF.

There are a number of recruitment agencies that recruit TEFL teachers. They are often looking for people with qualifications and experience. Write in with a CV and then follow up with a phone call. These agencies include those listed overleaf.

Centre for British Teachers
Quality House
Gyosei Campus
London Road
Reading
Berkshire RG1 5AQ
Telephone: 01734 756200

The Federation of Recruitment and Employment Services
36–38 Mortimer Street
London W1N 7RB
Telephone: 0171-323 4300

Produces a list of teaching agencies. Write with an SAE to the Education Department.

ILC Recruitment
International House
White Rock
Hastings
East Sussex TN34 1JY
Telephone: 01424 720100

Worldwide Education Services Consultancy
Canada House
272 Field End Road
Eastcote
Middlesex HA4 9NA
Telephone: 0181-866 4400

For more information on particular countries, contact the relevant embassies listed in the Country Index in Part 5.

Central Bureau for Educational Visits and Exchanges

Central Bureau is the UK national office for information and advice on all forms of educational visits and exchanges. As well as running a wide range of programmes, some of which are listed below, the Bureau also publishes books, information guides and newsletters and answers well over 30,000 enquiries every year. Its services are provided for teachers, lecturers and educationalists as well as pupils and anyone interested in gaining experience of other countries and cultures. Publications available cater for the needs of people seeking information on the various opportunities available for educational contacts and travel abroad.

For more information, contact Central Bureau at Seymour Mews, London W1H 9PE (telephone: 0171-486 5101).

English Language Assistants Programme

This programme places UK students and teachers in schools and colleges abroad. The role of the assistant is to help the teacher of English and, in particular, to help improve pupils' oral and aural skills, and to present aspects of the anglophone culture they represent. Graduates and undergraduates of any discipline, who are aged 20–30, native speakers of English and who have a knowledge of the relevant language at least to A-level or equivalent can apply. Modern language undergraduates can take a year out as a language assistant after two years of their degree.

Placements are usually available in eastern Europe, France, Germany, Italy, Spain and Latin America. Priority is given to undergraduates for placements in France, Germany, Italy and Spain and application is usually made via the university though graduates can also apply direct to Central Bureau. Application should be made between September and 1 December in the year prior to the placement. Placements usually start in September and last for the academic year. There is a lot of competition for placements; early application is advisable.

Those who apply for the placements in Latin America need a minimum of Spanish A-level or equivalent and many have a Spanish degree. For placements in eastern Europe, preference is given to graduates who have a TEFL qualification or TEFL experience. Candidates should apply from September to 1 December in the year prior to the placement. Applications may be accepted after the December closing date. Duties commence between July and September.

English language summer schools

British teachers and sixth-formers are recruited every year to participate in summer camps in Hungary, Poland and Turkey. Work in the camps includes helping with English teaching and organising activities (eg sport, music, social events, drama, art). Those who go meet new people and learn about the country, its way of life and culture. The camps usually begin in late July and last 3–4 weeks.

Applicants should be native speakers of English with a sense of responsibility, organisational skills, adaptability, a sociable personality, experience of working with children and an interest in sports and/or drama and music. Those who are interested should apply before January/early February in the year they want to go. Successful applicants receive free board and lodging but have to pay their own air fare.

Finnish family programme

Young people between 18–23 can go to Finland for between two or three months to 18 months to learn about the Finnish way of life. In return for free board and lodging and some pocket money, they teach English to the family they are living with and help with housework, childcare or outdoor work (eg farm work if they are living on a farm). Those on the programme usually work 25 hours over a five-day week. Applicants pay for their own air fare. Those who are interested in going to Finland in June/July need to apply to Central Bureau by early February in the year they want to go.

Junior language assistants programme

These opportunities are suitable for young people aged 18–20 years who are taking A-levels or other advanced-level qualifications in French, German or Spanish and who want to take a year out between school and higher education. Posts as junior language assistants are available in schools in France, Germany and Spain. The language assistants help with English tuition in schools 12 hours a week and receive board and lodging and a small allowance. They must, however, pay for their own air fare. The positions are usually available for six months. Early application is advisable as competition is fierce.

Teachers for Lithuania

The English language is of vital importance to this country, the largest of the Baltic states, which is striving to restore cultural, scientific and commercial links with western Europe. Motivation to study English in Lithuania is very high. There is, however, a great shortage of language teachers.

Teachers of English from the UK are welcomed in all schools in Lithuania. The Ministry of Culture and Education of the Republic of Lithuania arranges placement for graduates, of any discipline, from the UK, with or without teacher training. The employment contract is signed with the school.

The school provides free accommodation, free healthcare as covered by the Lithuanian Social Security Scheme (with an option of purchasing health insurance on an individual basis) and a salary equivalent to that of a Lithuanian teacher (approximately £50 per month which is enough to live on). Currently, there are no allowances for travelling expenses. The minimum teaching period preferred by the Ministry is one academic year of three terms.

To apply, send a letter of application and a CV including the names of two referees and a small photograph to the Teacher Training Department, Ministry of Culture and Education, Volano g. 2/7, 2691 Vilnius, Lithuania (telephone: 00 370 2 622483). A letter of placement will come directly from the Ministry to the applicant. There is no closing date for applications, but it is recommended that you apply by the end of March. The school year begins on 1 September and teachers should arrive, if possible, no later than 25 August.

Teachers in Greece

This is an organisation that provides English language teachers for private language institutes in Athens, Thessaloniki, provincial towns and on the islands. These institutes are mainly for children aged 8–18 and only a few in the larger towns cater for adults. Most children attend one of these institutes at some time during their school career. The institutes usually operate in the evenings from 4pm until 10pm, although some do have morning lessons from 10am until 12pm. The timing of the lessons fits in with children's attendance at state schools.

As the institutes are in the private sector, conditions and terms offered vary considerably. Many of the teaching posts are suitable for recently qualified teachers or graduates who are looking for a year or two of experience in teaching English as a foreign language. Some of the institutes, however, do demand TEFL experience and qualifications and salaries vary according to the specific requirements of the institute. The average salary is approximately £120 per week and often accommodation and flights are paid for by the employer, or accommodation is subsidised. Contracts are usually from September to the end of May/mid-June (minimum nine months). About 100 teachers are recruited each year and posts usually involve 25 hours of teaching per week. Some institutes organise summer schools in June, July and August and separate contacts can be negotiated for these months.

Those interested should apply by Easter in the year they intend to go. To apply, send CV and photo to the head office at Teachers in Greece, Taxilou 79, 20 Graphou 15771, Athens, Greece (telephone: 00 30 1 7792587).

Elizabeth Macadie

TEFL case-study

Elizabeth is studying modern Greek and Byzantine Studies at King's College, University of London. For most of the 1980s, she was teaching English in Greece.

‘After A-levels, I went on to train as a music teacher and, during my course, I spotted an advert for someone to teach English in Greece. The job involved teaching children in a family for two-and-a-half months in the summer vacation. I decided to apply and was offered the job. I enjoyed the job and this short experience made me think about doing TEFL for a longer period after teacher training.

After my course, I was offered a job in a school in Greece in Argos on the east coast of the Peleponnese. I taught English here for about two-and-a-half years. The children were between the ages of 6–17 years and I found them responsive and well-behaved. I didn't have a TEFL qualification but obviously knew how to teach. I followed the Michigan Proficiency Course and picked up knowledge of how to teach English grammar as I went along. I used role-play, dialogue, songs and shows to make the learning as much fun as possible.

After two-and-a-half years, I decided to set up my own language school in Kiveri, the village where I was living. I started off with six pupils and ended up with 65. I used the Cambridge proficiency syllabus and books. At this point, I was married to a Greek man and living with his family.

My marriage didn't work out and, in 1990, I returned to the UK on my own. However, I have no regrets about spending time in Greece. I thoroughly enjoyed myself and learnt a great deal. Obviously, I can now speak Greek fluently and I learnt a lot about dealing with people. I also learnt that you need to negotiate in a different way in a different culture and to be prepared to make compromises.

In another country, you have to learn to be independent, to take the rough with the smooth and to laugh at yourself. You learn to put yourself in other people's positions and to accept different attitudes. I now feel that I will be able to cope with most life experiences that are thrown at me.

I found the culture in Greece very different to the UK. The family and religion both play a strong part in people's lives and people don't tend to move from where they were born. I experienced a real culture shock when I returned to the UK after ten years in Greece. I found it strange going into pubs and I'd never seen cash machines before! I have quickly adjusted, though, and I'm now enjoying student life again.

I would recommend TEFL to people who are interested but would advise people to be open-minded and not to compare the country visited to the UK. What people should also think about is what they want to do when they return to the UK since returning and rethinking your career direction can be difficult. I feel that up to two years is a good time to spend teaching English abroad. ❞

For those with qualifications and experience

Voluntary Service Overseas runs the following programme for those who already have relevant qualifications or experience.

Voluntary Service Overseas – East European Partnership (EEP)

EEP was set up in 1990 to provide volunteers with particular skills in education and health in eastern Europe. EEP has identified several programmes through which volunteers can best help this area of Europe. These programmes are listed below.

English Teachers in Teacher Training Colleges

These programmes train English language teachers in the Baltic states, the Czech Republic, Poland and Slovakia.

Teachers of English for Special Purposes in Tertiary Colleges in Hungary

Volunteers teach English to groups of students at a variety of tertiary institutions.

The minimum qualifications required for the above two programmes are an arts degree, a TEFL certificate and/or PGCE, and two years' classroom experience.

Subject Teachers in Bi-lingual Schools

Trained humanities and maths/science teachers, who have taught up to A-level or equivalent, are needed to work closely with Czech and Slovak colleagues.

Health Promotion

EEP is looking for people from a number of professional backgrounds, including experienced youth and community/social workers, nurses and doctors involved with community health, to be based in regional health agencies in Romania.

Business Advisers

EEP is looking for people with qualifications in management, finance or marketing, with experience in the small enterprise sector, to advise Regional Business Agencies in Albania.

Volunteers have the security of an agreed salary and proper accommodation. EEP also provides a benefits package, travel costs, language training and professional support.

For more information, contact East European Partnership, Carlton House, 27a Carlton Drive, London SW15 2BS (telephone: 0181-780 2841, fax: 0181-780 9592).

You will also find organisations mentioned in chapter 12 that offer TEFL opportunities.

Work placements

The main opportunities for work placements abroad are via the IAESTE and AIESEC programmes, which organise placements for students during their degree courses. Students can also spend time on placements abroad via the European Union's Leonardo, Tempus and Socrates programmes. These programmes are explained in more detail below.

Leonardo

Between 1990 and 1994, the European Union's Petra action 1 and Comett programmes funded placements in Europe for students at college, in initial vocational training or at university. The European Union's new Leonardo programme for vocational training, which began on 1 January 1995, rationalises the EU's original training activities and builds on the achievements and positive aspects of Petra and Comett. The budget for Leonardo is ECU620 million (approximately £477 million) and the programme will run from 1995 to 1999.

Transnational placements and exchange programmes for young people, such as those previously supported under Petra action 1, will be funded under strand 1 of

Leonardo. These programmes are targeted at those in initial training, young workers, the unemployed and teaching staff. Placements will range from three weeks to one year. Transnational placements in firms for undergraduates for the purpose of technological development, such as those previously supported under Comett, will be funded under strand 2 of Leonardo. Placements will last for between three and 12 months.

For more details on Leonardo, contact the Department of Employment, Steel House, Tothill Street, London SW1H 9NF.

Tempus

Tempus is the Trans-European Co-operation Scheme for Higher Education and forms part of the overall EU programmes for the economic and social restructuring of central and eastern Europe (known as the PHARE programme) and for economic reform and recovery in the newly independent states of the former Soviet Union (known as the TACIS programme). The second stage of Tempus (PHARE) and Tempus (TACIS) began in the academic year 1994/5 and will run for four years.

Tempus (PHARE) can fund practical and study placements for students (not first-years) in eligible countries, which are Albania, Bulgaria, the Czech Republic, Estonia, Hungary, Latvia, Lithuania, Poland, Romania, Slovakia and Slovenia. Placements must relate to the national priority areas set up for each eligible country.

Under Tempus (TACIS), recent graduates may be able to serve as teachers in an eligible country. These countries are Armenia, Azerbaijan, Belarus, Georgia, Kazakhstan, Kyrgyzstan, Moldova, Mongolia, the Russian Federation, the Ukraine and Uzbekistan.

Details on Tempus are available from the Europe Higher Education Unit, British Council, Medlock Street, Manchester M15 4AA (telephone: 0161-957 7074/5/6).

Socrates

Under the EU's new programme for education, Socrates, which will run from 1995 to 1999, assistantships abroad for those training to be language teachers will be encouraged.

For more information, contact the Lingua unit, Central Bureau, Seymour Mews, London W1H 9PF (telephone: 0171-486 5101).

AIESEC UK

AIESEC is a French acronym and is an international association of students of economics and business management. It is a non-profit-making student organisation that is run and managed by students and recent university graduates. AIESEC was established in 1948 and comprises over 700 universities in 81 member countries and is expanding to include China, Sri Lanka and Vietnam. It has a membership of 60,000, which includes members from most of the European countries.

AIESEC organises an international work experience programme called the International Traineeship Exchange Programme (ITEP). This is for students of business studies, management, marketing, finance, economics, accounts and other business-related subjects. Each year approximately 6,000 student from the 81 countries involved take part in a work experience placement abroad.

AIESEC UK is made up of student committees at 31 universities scattered throughout the UK. These universities are Aberdeen, Aston, Birmingham, Bournemouth, Bristol, Cambridge, Cardiff, City and Guildhall, East Anglia, Edinburgh, Exeter, Hull, Kent, Leeds, Liverpool, London School of Economics, Loughborough, Manchester, Newcastle, Nottingham, Oxford, Portsmouth, Queen's (Belfast), Reading, Sheffield, Southampton, St Andrews, Stirling, Strathclyde, University of Jordan (Ulster) and Warwick.

The student committees at all the universities are involved in raising placements with employers in their area for students from abroad, and in looking after the students while they are on their placement. For every placement that the university committee raises in the UK, a student from that institution can be sent on a placement abroad.

Placements can last from eight weeks to 18 months and take place all year round (in a summer holiday, a year out during the degree or after graduation). Students who want to apply for a placement need to become involved in their local AIESEC committee before applying. Each year, approximately 400 students, or graduates, from the UK take up placements abroad. There is a fair amount of competition for places. Applications are considered by the local committee and the AIESEC head office in the UK and they are then sent to Brussels for a computer-matching process. Students who undertake placements are paid a minimum wage which is standard in the country and which is enough to cover accommodation and living expenses. Students pay for their own flight and their accommodation is arranged by the AIESEC committee in the area they are going to.

For more information, contact AIESEC UK, National HQ, 29–31 Cowper Street, London EC2A 4AP (telephone: 0171-336 7939).

IAESTE

The International Association for the Exchange of Students for Technical Experience (IAESTE) is an independent worldwide organisation for which the Central Bureau is the UK office. Northern Ireland IAESTE operates independently. IAESTE provides course-related paid work experience placements abroad for science, agriculture, horticulture, architecture, engineering, computer science and applied arts degree students. There are now 64 countries that are members of IAESTE and, since 1948, over 250,000 students have gained work experience through the programme.

Most placements are from 6–12 weeks from May to October (some placements can be up to a year) and students at British universities who are interested in the scheme need to apply to Central Bureau from September to December in the year before they would like to do their work experience. There is a placement fee of £48.

Students taking part in the programme are usually in their second or third year of higher education. IAESTE national offices find accommodation for incoming students and students receive a salary while they are working. Students do, however, have to pay their air fare.

For more information on IAESTE, contact Central Bureau, Seymour Mews, London W1H 9PE (telephone: 0171-725 9459).

Zentralstelle für Arbeitsvermittlung

ZAV can find two- to three-month summer posts for students aged 18–30. Applicants should have A-level German or equivalent and be able to provide proof of university enrolment; otherwise they will be liable for tax and national insurance contributions. Time-out placements in Germany are organised with help from ZAV.

For more information, write to Zentralstelle für Arbeitsvermittlung, Postfach 17 05 45, 60079 Frankfurt am Main, Germany. If you are in Germany, the visiting address is Feuerbachstrasse 42–46, 60325 Frankfurt am Main (telephone: 00 49 69 71 110).

As well as the above programmes, there are many other possibilities which you can look into for your time out before, during or after university, or as a break from employment. These opportunities could be in the European Union countries, EFTA countries or in eastern Europe (eg Hungary, Czech and Slovak Republics). They could also be closer to home.

Horizon HPL

Horizon HPL arranges work placements for Europeans in hotels, restaurants and commercial companies in France and the UK. It also runs complementary language training courses in Paris. For more information on the hotel work placements, see the section on working in the tourist industry. The primary aim of the placements is for people to improve their language skills, while at the same time gaining valuable work experience.

The majority of applicants are 17–30. For placements in France, applicants are invited to interview and undergo a French test. Formal qualifications in French are not required but, at the minimum, a basic knowledge of the language is required.

Placements in companies include secretarial, accounting and marketing positions. Horizon will also bear in mind other ideas applicants may have and will try to find a suitable placement. Placements can last from three to 12 months and applicants for these placements need a good understanding of French. Previous experience may be required, eg for secretarial placements. Trainees placed in companies are usually paid £30 a week and have to pay for their own accommodation which Horizon can find for them. On average, accommodation will cost FF2,000 (about £250) a month. Trainees are expected to support themselves while on work placements.

Horizon charges a fee of £300 for work placements. For further information, contact Horizon HPL, Black Prince Road, London SE1 7SJ (telephone: 0171-735 8171).

Working as a sales representative

Currently, one organisation offers opportunities for young people from the UK to work as sales representatives, in Italy.

Mercury Enterprises (Italia)

Mercury Enterprises (Italia) is a registered Italian company selling language courses and reference books to business people. Young people, aged 17–25, are invited to join its small sales groups travelling throughout Italy. Sales experience is not necessary as full training is provided on arrival in Italy. A prior knowledge of Italian is helpful, though not essential, but all applicants must be keen to learn the language.

Sales representatives obtain orders by calling on business and professional people (eg shopkeepers, manufacturers, artisans and teachers). Italians enjoy meeting overseas visitors and find it interesting to deal with a foreign salesperson. Approximately 40 people are recruited for these positions each year. The minimum length of service is six months and there is no set maximum.

Accommodation is provided by the company in small family-run hotels; meals are not included. Groups travel by car and usually spend between two to three weeks in each area. Working for Mercury offers good commission and bonuses and an opportunity to see a lot of Italy and learn Italian while gaining on-the-road sales experience during a gap year. Non-smokers only are accepted. Apply with CV and passport photo to Miss Manoli, Mercury Enterprises (Italia), 13 Castle Hill Avenue, Folkestone, Kent CT20 2TD.

Following are comments from three girls who recently went to Italy with Mercury Enterprises.

Susan Peterborough

‘I spent six months in Sardinia when I was 20 and made about £4,000 which paid for a trip to Australia. I didn't know much Italian before I went, just basic greetings, but was fairly fluent after six months. It's hard speaking Italian to begin with but you learn a sales talk and spend the first few weeks learning how to sell by going out with an experienced person.

It's hard work and you need to be determined and confident. It is fun and good experience but definitely not a holiday job. You have to be prepared to put in a lot of effort and at the end of the day you feel pretty tired. I would recommend it, though, and feel that I can do anything now.’

Sinead McGovern

‘I went to Italy when I was 23 and spent almost a year and a half with Mercury Enterprises. I made a lot of money and learnt to speak Italian very quickly. You travel all over Italy in a group of about six and you see a lot of the country. I was older than most of the people in the group and, being more independent, I had to learn to compromise. I didn't have a problem selling but this does depend on your personality. You have to be outgoing, to like selling and to want to make money. It's also important that you're not afraid of hard work and that you like Italy, travelling, learning about new cultures and meeting new people. I loved it, it's a great way to see Italy and to travel the country but you must be the right type of person for the work. '

Arabella Hall

' I went to Italy with Mercury Enterprises for about a year. I was homesick at first but later on I thoroughly enjoyed myself. To begin with, there is a pressure to learn the language but you manage to pick up what you need fairly quickly. I wasn't particularly good at the pronunciation but used this to my advantage. The clients would spend time with me teaching the correct pronunciation and the longer you are with a client the more likely you are to make a sale. It sounds odd but somehow you can sell with a very basic knowledge of Italian.

I think everyone should have a little adventure before they settle down to study or employment. I'm not that confident but when I was away I could cover that up since the people I was with had no expectations as to how I would behave. It's very important to have a year out and to have a stab at independence. I loved Italy. It's so beautiful and I loved the shopping and the food. I also made some strong friendships and found the experience character-building. '

Farm work

All sorts of agricultural jobs are available for those aged 16 plus. Perhaps the greatest number of opportunities are available in fruit-picking. This can be back-breaking work and poor weather affects the amount of work available.

There are more details on this kind of work in Part 5.

Fruit-picking

Fruit-picking is a popular form of casual work in France starting with soft fruit in early summer and going on to the grape harvest in September/October. Work can be found throughout France. ANPE (see under France in the Country Index in Part 5) is notified of some vacancies and it is also worth asking on farms.

Where else can you look for employment?

Below, you will find details of other sources of employment opportunities in continental Europe.

EURES

There is now a system of exchanging vacancies between the 15 countries of the European Union. This system is called EURES (European Employment Services). In the UK, it is possible to access a database of European vacancies via Jobcentres and there are also several Euro-advisers working at bases throughout the UK. They are regularly in touch with their counterparts abroad and can give people advice about working and living in other European countries. They can also put you in touch with the Employment Service in the country you want to go to.

For more information, contact your local Jobcentre or the Overseas Placing Unit (OPU) in Sheffield which is the UK co-ordinator of the EURES network.

The OPU has produced a series of fact sheets on working in all the European Union countries. It is based at 4th Floor, Skills House, 3–7 Holy Green, The Moor, Sheffield S1 4AQ (telephone: 0114 259 6051/2). Please write in for information.

Job vacancies in newspapers

When looking for a job from the UK, you may want to consult the newspaper *Overseas Jobs Express* (to subscribe, contact *Overseas Jobs Express*, PO Box 22,

Brighton, East Sussex BN1 6HX) or the magazine *Jobs International* (available from Cromwell Court, New Road, St Ives, Cambridgeshire PE17 4BG). Both of the above have advertisements for jobs available in Europe and worldwide. Jobs include long- and short-term positions such as fruit-picking, working on cruise liners, working in ski resorts, hotel work, etc.

Using Employment Services

It is possible to find paid work in Europe by using the Employment Service in the country you wish to visit and by looking in the local newspapers. If you decide to do this, you will need to be fairly confident that you have good enough written and spoken skills in the language to be able to hold down a job. For the other 14 countries of the European Union, you will not need a work permit. If you have been claiming social security benefits in the UK for a minimum of four weeks, you can also claim this benefit for up to three months while you look for work in another EU country. For those countries outside the Union you will need to contact the embassy concerned for work permit information. Before leaving the UK, check the unemployment situation with the embassy of the country you are planning to visit. Many countries, particularly in southern and eastern Europe, are still facing the crisis of mass unemployment.

12 Work in the Community

There are many organisations throughout Europe offering opportunities for young people to take part in voluntary work projects. Volunteers usually pay for their own travel but accommodation is provided free. Sometimes meals are provided free and volunteers may also be given pocket money. Applicants need to show a strong commitment to the type of work they are applying for. The minimum age for projects varies and can be as low as 12 years. However, the majority of organisations recruit people who are over 18. Sometimes there is a maximum age limit of 25 or 30.

The work carried out varies from project to project. A few examples include social work, working with poor, deprived and disadvantaged individuals and families, teaching English as a foreign language and office work. Volunteers work from a few weeks up to more than a year; some organisations prefer volunteers to commit themselves to a longer period of time. Usually no experience is required and training will often be given. For TEFL positions, however, a qualification or experience may be required. In continental Europe, proficiency in a foreign language may sometimes be needed.

Many organisations recruit volunteers from all over Europe and/or the world which means that volunteers usually work, and make friends, with other people of many nationalities. However, individuals may be sent to work alone on a project and be found local accommodation. Some voluntary activities take place on workcamps where volunteers live in close contact with each other sharing the cooking, shopping and other chores. Living conditions can be basic. On workcamps particularly, social, leisure and sports activities are often organised for participants.

Voluntary work is a challenging way of spending a

year out. It offers you the opportunity to put something back into the wider community, to meet people from other nations, to learn about another country and culture, to learn about yourself and to develop personal skills. It can be extremely rewarding and you can make friends for life. It also looks very good on a CV or university UCAS form. Through voluntary work, it is possible to gain experience which may be essential for some professions and which will improve your chances of entering others. People considering entering social and health careers can boost their careers via voluntary work in the community in the UK, or abroad.

Short-term voluntary work in the community can be of great benefit to people socially and educationally and there are many opportunities to participate actively in improving community life. Examples of projects include helping to run play schemes for able-bodied or disabled children, helping the elderly, working with immigrant communities and taking children from deprived inner city areas on holiday in the countryside. Volunteers usually receive board and lodging and may be given pocket money and travel expenses. Projects are run at Christmas and Easter as well as in the summer vacation. Volunteers usually need to be at least 18 years. Details of organisations that offer young people the opportunity to do voluntary work in the community are listed below.

ATD Fourth World

ATD is an international, voluntary organisation which works alongside the poorest, most disadvantaged and excluded families, in an effort to protect and guarantee their fundamental rights, including the right to family life, education and representation.

The organisation recruits full-time coreworkers who commit themselves on a long-term basis (minimum two years) and agree to work in any of the teams in the Americas, Africa, Asia or Europe. These coreworkers support the efforts of the poor in overcoming extreme poverty and taking an active role in their community. No skills or qualifications are required as volunteers receive training in the UK first.

For those interested in a short-term commitment, there is a three-month, full-time introductory programme, which takes place in London and/or Surrey. This involves manual and office work, assisting in projects with poor families, and learning about ATD Fourth World through talks, books, videos and discussions. Normally between two and five people take part and find it an enjoyable time and a great learning experience. After this programme people can decide to make a commitment of at least two years, or to join one of the teams in Europe for a shorter period.

Alternatively, workcamps are arranged in Britain and France. Here, volunteers help out with building, decorating, gardening and secretarial work and, at the same time, learn about the organisation through talks and discussions. Volunteers can also work directly with the families; activities such as Street Workshops and Respite Stays take place in Britain and Europe throughout the year. All these events last approximately two weeks.

Before taking part in any of these activities, ATD Fourth World prefers potential volunteers to attend a working weekend in London or Surrey. Applicants must be 18 years and above. No particular experience, skills or qualifications are required. However, applicants should be interested in gaining a better understanding of the causes and effects of persistent poverty, and be willing to work hard with others as part of a team. The minimum length of service is two weeks.

Volunteers on workcamps and those taking part in other activities contribute towards the cost of food and accommodation. Those who take part in the three-month introductory programme receive accommodation for the whole programme and a basic wage for the second and third months but they must contribute towards the cost of food.

For more information, write enclosing an SAE to the

Director, ATD Fourth World, 48 Addington Square, London SE5 7LB (telephone: 0171-703 3231).

The Baptist Missionary Society (BMS)

The Action Teams offer opportunities for those aged 18–25 years to find out about life in a different country, share in practical work with a local Baptist church and be involved in their mission to the community around them.

From mid-September, teams of six get a month's training, then a full six months living in another part of the world followed by two months back in Britain sharing their experiences with churches and youth groups.

In Europe, teams can go to France and Italy. Teams also go to other parts of the world. For more details, see chapter 17 in Part 4. Participants contribute to travel and training expenses. BMS provides accommodation within Britain and the partner country.

For more information, contact the Missionary Support Manager, The Baptist Missionary Society, PO Box 49, Baptist House, 129 Broadway, Didcot, Oxfordshire OX11 8RT (telephone: 01235 512077).

Concordia (Youth Service Volunteers)

Concordia (Youth Service Volunteers) works with European voluntary youth organisations which organise international workcamps in western, central and eastern Europe, Turkey and Tunisia. Camps last 2–3 weeks and take place from the end of June until mid-September. Most of the projects are concerned with nature conservation, environmental protection and the restoration of monuments and castles, but some offer community and social work, counselling on children's camps or English-language teaching. For more information, see chapter 13 on conservation work.

GAP Activity Projects

GAP organises voluntary work opportunities for 18–19 year olds during their 'gap' year between school/college and higher education or employment. It aims to broaden young people's horizons by giving them the opportunity to do charitable-type work in another country. Work attachments are for 6–9 months and include helping the sick, disabled and deprived, English language teaching, assisting in schools, conservation, farming and office work in 33 different countries around the world (including Europe).

Applicants pay a £20 registration fee and, on selection, a fee to GAP of £395 (1994/5). A one- or two-week TEFL course (approximately £100–£150) is also required for those who choose or are selected to do English teaching. Volunteers receive free board and lodging and, in most cases, some pocket money at their placements, but are responsible for their own return air fares, insurance and medical costs.

Claire Ferry

GAP Activity Projects case-study

Claire is now at university studying Natural Sciences and Hungarian. In her year out she spent some of her time in Hungary teaching English via GAP Activity Projects' programme.

'After my A-levels, I taught English in Hungary via GAP's programme. I wanted an adventure, to become more independent, to see new places and meet new people and to improve my spoken German, which I had studied at A-level.

I originally applied for a placement in Germany but ended up in Hungary. I am glad that it worked out this way as I feel that the Hungarian experience was more fulfilling and exciting than the German one would have been.

I worked as a teaching assistant in Budapest for five months and then spent a month travelling around Slovakia, Poland and Romania. I was based in a comprehensive school for children aged 14–18, teaching 14 lessons a week. I took 11 classes once a week, sharing them with Hungarian teachers. I was there as a native speaker and organised activities such as role-plays, discussions and games to encourage the students to speak English. I also had one group which I took on my own and saw three times a week. I taught them from a course book provided by the school and also used some of my own ideas. I also helped run the English Club where I organised games and discussions and helped students with homework or English conversation.

The school was a bit disorganised but all the staff were very helpful and kind and ready to help me with any problems I might have. I was the first GAP student they had taken. I communicated mainly in German or English and also picked up quite a lot of Hungarian. I was keen to learn Hungarian and had a few lessons. Occasionally, it would have been useful for me to have known more Hungarian in the teaching situation (particularly when standing in front of a group of rowdy 14 year olds) but, generally, I encountered few problems. Before I went to Hungary I took a one-week TEFL course run by English Worldwide in Concordia Wharf. This was arranged by GAP. GAP insists all volunteers going abroad to teach English do this course before they go.

I lived in accommodation found by the school. This was a girls' hostel where meals were provided during the week and I cooked for myself at weekends. I was paid the equivalent of about £110 a month plus given food vouchers to use at a major chain of supermarkets. I could live comfortably on this and I also managed to save about £40 a month.

Everyone in Hungary was friendly, open and generous and I made lots of friends who I will keep in touch with. I also met the nine other GAP students in Hungary and saw them later on when I travelled around Romania, Poland and Slovakia.

I thoroughly enjoyed my time in eastern Europe and now feel more independent and confident. I managed in a foreign country where I didn't speak the language. I did more travelling and met more people than I had expected to and now feel that I could have a go at anything. I would recommend a year out but would add that what you achieve is down to you. You need to go with an open mind, not expect anything and be prepared to use your own initiative.

After returning from Hungary, I worked as a care assistant in a nursing home for a short time and then went to Germany and worked on an organic farm for two-and-a-half months. After this, I hitch-hiked around Europe for two months. ❜

For further information, please write to GAP Activity Projects, GAP House, 44 Queen's Road, Reading, Berkshire RG1 4BB (telephone: 01734 594914).

Internationale Jugendgemeinschaftsdienste EV

This German organisation runs workcamps in Germany and other parts of the world. A variety of work is available ranging from renovating old buildings and gardening to social work helping children and old people. Volunteers pay their own travel costs and a small fee, DEM150 (approximately £60) for camps in Germany and DEM230 (approximately £90) for camps elsewhere, which covers their food and accommodation. Volunteers can work from between two to four weeks and most workcamps take place in the summer. Applicants for German camps should be 16 and above; for the other camps they should be 18 and above.

For more information, contact Internationale Jugendgemeinschaftsdienste EV, Kaiserstrasse 43, 53113 Bonn, Germany (telephone: 00 49 228 22 10 01)

International Voluntary Service

IVS runs workcamps throughout Europe. There are a few opportunities for medium-term voluntary work in Europe after workcamp participation. For more information see chapter 8 in Part 2.

Nansen International Centre, Norway

Breivold is a long-term relief centre for teenagers ranging from 13–18 years old with deep social and emotional needs. It is situated on a renovated farm 25 km from Oslo. Help is needed in all aspects of the centre. Applicants with skills of a practical nature and with the initiative to tackle and follow through ideas with the minimum of supervision are needed. Domestic and farm work is also included in the rota, with all volunteers taking turns to cook. Cleaning duties and care of the animals are part of the daily routine at Breivold.

There are many possibilities for sports, hobbies, trips, etc and leaders are expected to motivate the youths in all areas of life. This is the most important aspect of the work as it prepares the young people at the centre for the future.

Volunteers at Breivold must be willing to work very hard as the hours are both long and tiring. Volunteers should preferably be over 22, qualified drivers and have some experience of working with young people. Volunteers receive full board and lodging and Nkr500 (approximately £50) per week. Applicants are expected to stay a year. There is also a special summer project lasting for six weeks, for which the application deadline is the end of March. It takes between three and six months to process the necessary work permits.

Send an international reply coupon for all correspondence or you may not receive a reply. Apply to the Director at Nansen International Centre, Barnegården, Breivold, Nesset–1433 Vinterbro, Norway (telephone: 00 47 64946791/15).

Toc H

Toc H is a Christian society, originally founded to combat loneliness among British soldiers, which now engages in a wide range of social work in the English-speaking world. As well as a number of schemes in Britain, Toc H runs projects in Germany where volunteers provide a range of services to British service personnel and their families based there, for example bookshops, a canteen and accommodation facilities. Recent projects include helping Santa on his tour of Toc H centres around Germany and helping to prepare the Toc H contribution to the German Flower Festival. A fee is charged which goes towards transport and volunteers require their own spending money.

The minimum age for applicants is 18; there is no maximum age. Those who have experience of working with children and/or experience of Toc H projects in the UK are given preference. There is no closing date for applications but it is advisable to apply early as only a small number of people are recruited each year.

Further details can be found in the Toc H Projects Programme, published twice yearly on the first Monday of March and September. For more information, contact National Projects Co-ordinator, Toc H, 1 Forest Close, Wendover, Aylesbury, Buckinghamshire HP22 6BT (telephone: 01296 623911, fax: 01296 696137).

13 Conservation and Renovation Work

Voluntary conservation and renovation work is a challenging way of spending a year out. It offers you the opportunity to put something back into the wider community, to meet people from other nations, to learn about another country and culture, to learn about yourself and to develop personal skills. It is hard work and can involve long hours and you will need to be physically fit; you need to show enthusiasm and to know something about the area you choose to go to. The minimum age for projects varies but the majority of organisations recruit people who are over 18. Sometimes there is a maximum age limit of 25 or 30.

The work is usually practical in nature such as building, gardening, land-clearing, environmental protection, conservation and farming work, building renovation and disaster reconstruction but can include administrative work. Volunteers work from a few weeks up to more than a year; some organisations prefer volunteers to commit themselves to a longer period of time. Usually no experience is required and training will often be given.

Many organisations recruit volunteers from all over Europe and/or the world which means that volunteers usually work, and make friends, with other people of many nationalities. However, individuals may be sent to work alone on a project and be found local accommodation. Some voluntary activities take place on workcamps where volunteers live in close contact with each other sharing the cooking, shopping and other chores. Living conditions can be basic. On workcamps particularly, social, leisure and sports activities are often organised for participants.

Volunteering can look very good on a CV or university UCAS form. Through voluntary work, it is possible to gain experience which may be essential for some professions and which will improve your chances of entering others. People considering conservation or environmental work can boost their careers via voluntary experience in the UK, or abroad.

Bouworde Flanders

Bouworde Flanders in Belgium organises three types of voluntary work to implement construction projects for people who need help. These are:

1. Workcamps during the school holidays
2. Projects for long-term volunteers
3. Projects for the Telebouworde (voluntary work in your free time).

1 Workcamps

These take place during the months of July, August and September. Bouworde Flanders organises workcamps (usually three weeks) in Belgium and in Austria, the Czech Republic, France, Germany, Hungary, Italy, Lithuania, Poland, Romania, Russia, Slovak Republic, Spain, and the Ukraine. During the Christmas and Easter holidays, Bouworde Flanders organises short workcamps of one week in Flanders.

Volunteers of different nationalities carry out all kinds of construction work (painting, wallpapering, sanitary works, bricklaying, joinery work, electrical work). They work eight hours a day, five days a week. Technical experience and/or skills are not required; volunteers are guided and supervised by a technical leader. In exchange for their work, volunteers get free accommodation and meals. Travel costs and insurance are at the volunteer's expense.

Anyone who is 18 years and above can participate. Volunteers should be prepared to participate in every aspect of workcamp life and to respect the prevailing culture of the country they are working in. Volunteers apply by filling in an application form and paying BF1500 (approximately £30).

2 Long-term volunteers

Volunteers who want to commit themselves for a longer period can work all year round on projects in Flanders. They carry out the same kind of work as the volunteers on workcamps. Sometimes the work is more specialised and the volunteers can gain more experience.

Usually there are two groups of volunteers, one working near Antwerp and the other near Brussels/Leuven. Long-term volunteers are made up of all kinds of people – the unemployed, students, people taking a break from their studies or careers, and retired people. There are no special preconditions and these people work on the same conditions as those for the workcamps – 40 hours a week work for free accommodation and meals. Applicants need to fill in an application form and pay BF1500.

3 Telebouworde (voluntary work in your free time)

People who want to help throughout the year but who are busy during the week can take part in Bouworde activities during the weekends (usually on Saturdays) in their own region. They carry out all kinds of jobs (not only construction work) for the elderly, the disabled and disadvantaged people in their region. Obviously, UK citizens can only take part in the Telebouworde if they are living and working in Belgium already and want to do voluntary work at the weekend.

For more information on any of these projects, contact either Bouworde vzw, Tiensesteenweg 145, Kessel-1, 3010 Leuven, Belgium (telephone: 00 32 16 25 91 44) or Compagnons Batisseurs, Rue des Carmes 24, 6900 Marche, Belgium (telephone: 00 32 84 31 44 13).

Bouworde also has offices in Austria, France, Germany, Hungary, Italy, The Netherlands and Switzerland that organise voluntary work.

Austria

Osterreichischer Bauorden
Hornesgasse 4
1031 Vienna
Telephone: 00 43 1 713 52 54

France

Compagnons Batisseurs
64 Rue Maillot
81100 Castres
Telephone: 00 33 63 72 59 64

Germany

Deutscher Bauorden
Liebigstrasse 23
6520 Worms-Horchheim
Telephone: 00 49 6241 31 95

Hungary

Epito Baratok
Edina Boglary Mailath
Blathy Otto u. 10
1089 Budapest
Telephone: 00 36 1 133 63 03

Italy

Soci Costruttori
Via Mazza 48
20071 Casalpusterlengo (MI)
Telephone: 00 39 377 84 988

The Netherlands

Bouworde Nederland
Sint Annastraat 172
6524 GT Nijmegen
Telephone: 00 31 80 22 60 74

Switzerland

Internationaler Bauorden
J. Feurer
Kirchweg
9438 Lucchingen
Telephone: 00 41 71 75 60 69

British Trust for Conservation Volunteers

BTCV recruits volunteers for conservation projects worldwide. For more information, see chapter 9 in Part 2.

Chantiers de Jeunes, Provence Côte d'Azur

This organisation offers voluntary work opportunities for those aged 14–17 years. Volunteers work five hours per day, six days per week for one week during the school year or two weeks in the summer. There are places for 14 volunteers (seven female, seven male). The work involves environmental protection and volunteers work on a 17th-century fort on the Isle Ste Marguerite (Cannes). Young people meet others of different nationalities and are responsible for doing their own food shopping, and preparing and cooking meals. There are watersports, games and shows in the afternoons and evenings. Volunteers pay their own travel and FF2,100 (approximately £250) for membership, food, accommodation, work, activities and insurance.

For more information, contact Chantiers de Jeunes Provence Côte d'Azur, Maison des Chantiers-Ferme Giaume, 7 avenue Pierre de Coubertin, 06150 Cannes-La Bocca, France (telephone: 00 33 93 47 89 69, fax: 00 33 93 48 12 01).

Concordia (Youth Service Volunteers)

Concordia (Youth Service Volunteers) is a non-profit-making charity which celebrated its 50th anniversary in 1993. It works in conjunction with European voluntary youth organisations which organise international work-camps in western, central and eastern Europe, Turkey and Tunisia. Camps last 2–3 weeks and take place from the end of June until mid-September. In addition to the summer workcamp programme, work can also be arranged on farms in Norway (for up to three months) and in the French- and German-speaking cantons of Switzerland (for up to two months in the period from March to November). Pocket money is paid in these cases.

Accommodation and conditions vary considerably from camp to camp, depending on the country and what is available. Youth hostels, school halls, farm cottages, mountain huts and tents are all used to accommodate volunteers at different camps. Volunteers must be prepared to cope with simple, often basic, conditions.

The nature of the work varies from camp to camp; many projects are concerned with nature conservation and environmental protection. Others provide work on the restoration of monuments and castles, construction, community and social work, counselling on children's camps and some English language teaching. As a rule, volunteers work a five- or five-and-a-half-day week, though the number of hours worked depends on the climate. Participating in a workcamp certainly challenges a volunteer's skills, inner resources and initiative and can also be excellent fun.

A registration fee is charged in all cases, but this varies greatly from country to country. As a guideline, fees in 1994 ranged between £50–£70. The registration fee covers board and lodging and, in most cases, insurance against accidents while at the camp. In addition, many camps make arrangements for sports and social activities and excursions out of hours and at weekends. Volunteers pay their own travel costs and are responsible for travel arrangements, visas, etc. Concordia prefers applicants to be flexible as the dates of the camps may change at short notice.

Applicants must be between 18 (17 for Germany) and 30 years old. In some cases, the upper age limit is 26. As the work is strenuous, physical fitness is essential. Volunteers are expected to participate in all aspects of camp life (cooking in turn for the whole group, for example). A working knowledge of a foreign language may be required but applicants without this should not be deterred. English is used as the language of communication at most camps. For many camps, previous voluntary workcamp experience is not required.

If you are interested in receiving a fact sheet, please send a small SAE to Overseas Volunteer Co-ordinator, Concordia (YSV) Ltd, 8 Brunswick Place, Hove, East Sussex BN3 1ET (telephone: 01273 772086).

Cotravaux

Cotravaux is a co-ordinating organisation of ten French and international associations, providing general information about them and promoting the voluntary work. The camps in France last for two or three weeks and revolve around social or manual work (renovation, construction, land-clearing, nature preservation, restoration of ancient monuments, archaeological digs, etc). The minimum age for volunteers on most camps is 18. However, some accept volunteers younger than this; a very few accept volunteers as young as 13.

For more information, contact Cotravaux at 11 rue de Clichy, 75009 Paris, France 75009 (telephone: 00 33 1 48 74 79 20).

Earthwatch Europe

Earthwatch Europe recruits volunteers for conservation projects worldwide. For more details, see chapter 9 in Part 2.

Emmaus International

Emmaus is an international movement made up of 350 communities and groups in 37 countries throughout the world. It aims at sharing with those living in moral and material misery, and fighting on both public and private levels against the causes of such destitution. The movement was originally set up in France but now operates throughout the world.

Emmaus International organises workcamps in Europe for 15 days a month or more. The camps are for people aged 18 and above who want to have a practical experience of sharing. The work involves reprocessing used objects (clothes, scrap and furniture), sorting, repairing and selling these items. Board and accommodation are usually provided.

For more information, contact Emmaus International, 183 bis rue Vaillant Couturrier, BP 91, F-94143 Alfortville, Cedex (telephone: 00 33 1 48 93 29 50).

GAP Activity Projects

GAP organises voluntary work opportunities, mostly in the community but occasionally on conservation projects. For more information, see chapter 12.

Gruppo Volontari Della Svizzera Italiana (GVSI)

The GVSI is a group consisting of adults and young people in the Italian part of Switzerland who welcome foreigners who want to take part in an international workcamp. At present, there are about 100 active members of the group. Volunteers must be 18 and above. Volunteers are involved in reconstruction and maintenance work after natural disasters and they are involved in helping the aged by, for example, cutting wood, helping in their homes, in stables, in orchards, etc. Group members allocate other work such as cooking, cleaning and shopping between them. Volunteers are given a house in the village to live in. Camps last from 1 June to 30 September and volunteers usually stay for one or two weeks.

For more information, contact Gruppo Volontari Della Svizzera Italiana (GVSI), C.P 12, 6517 Arbedo, Switzerland (telephone: 00 41 92 274520).

Internationale Jugendgemeinschaftsdienste EV

This German organisation runs conservation and social work volunteer workcamps in Germany and other parts of the world. For more details, see entry in chapter 12.

The Missions to Seamen

The Missions to Seamen organises voluntary opportunities in the shipping industry for young Christian men and women. Volunteers are based in 20 ports around the world in Europe, the Far East, Australia, the USA and Africa. Volunteers assist a port chaplain and work may involve visiting ships, practical work such as gardening, visiting hospitals, conducting sight-seeing tours, arranging sporting events, helping with worship, serving in the seafarers' centre's bar and shop, etc.

Applicants must be at least 18 and hold a valid driving licence. They should be Anglican or a member of another Christian denomination and be prepared to participate fully in Anglican ministry and worship. The average length of service is one year and 20 volunteers are recruited each year. Free board and accommodation are provided, travel fares are paid and volunteers receive about £30 per week. Overseas pay is adjusted to the cost of living.

Applications should ideally be made by the end of March to start July/August/September the same year. For more information, contact the Ministry Secretary, The Missions to Seamen, St Michael Paternoster Royal, College Hill, London EC4R 2RL (telephone: 0171-248 5202).

Natuur 2000

Natuur 2000 organises nature conservation workcamps. Volunteers can be involved in nature conservation, technical preparation and organisation of study and conservation camps and in administrative office jobs (computer work). Voluntary work is usually for between one week to one month. The minimum age for most activities is usually 12 or 14 years. Board and accommodation are provided (except for those who participate on nature conservation camps).

For more information, contact Natuur 2000, Bervoetstraat 33, B2000 Antwerpen, Belgium (telephone: 00 32 32 31 26 04).

pro international e.V

This German organisation offers unpaid voluntary work in international workcamps. Camp work can involve organising children's holidays, environmental work, renovation, etc. Volunteers usually stay 2–3 weeks and insurance, board and accommodation are free.

For more information, contact pro international e.V, Bahnhofstrasse 26A, 35037 Marburg, Germany (telephone: 00 49 6421 65277, fax: 00 49 6421 64407).

Other sources of voluntary work

It is also possible to find voluntary work abroad through friends, schools, colleges, churches and universities. Use your contacts and ask around. You may be able to get financial help from your local Rotary Club or another local charity or grant-giving organisation. Details of charitable and grant-making organisations can be found in your local library.

14 Study in Continental Europe

Another option to consider is spending time in Europe improving your language skills or studying a relevant course. Many graduate employers are now interested in applicants who have good language skills. Having language ability could mean that you stand out from others in the selection process. Studying abroad will also bring you into contact with people of different nationalities and will broaden your horizons. A number of organisations will offer you the opportunity to spend time improving your language ability abroad.

During higher education

By the end of 1994, more than 300,000 students had taken part in the European Union's Erasmus and Lingua higher-education study programmes. These programmes enabled students on degree and HND courses to spend between three months and a year studying abroad as part of their course. All universities and some colleges ran these programmes and a variety of vocational and academic subjects were offered. The Lingua programme concentrated on students who were spending at least 50 per cent of their time learning a language, or training to teach one.

From 1995, these programmes came under the umbrella of the European Union's new Socrates programme and they will continue in much the same way. Erasmus has been an extremely successful programme and in 1993/4 approximately 11,000–12,000 UK students took part in it.

The number of students taking part in Erasmus programmes is expected to increase yearly and not less than 55 per cent of the Socrates budget will be committed to Erasmus. Under Socrates, more efforts will be put into developing the ECTS (European Credit Transfer System) so that students receive credit for their time spent in another country.

The UK Erasmus Student Grants Council at the University of Kent will be co-ordinating the Erasmus part of Socrates, including higher education study periods previously under Lingua.

The Erasmus Student Grants Council is based at the University of Kent, Canterbury, Kent CT2 7PD (telephone: 01227 762712).

For more information about the development of Socrates, contact the Department for Education, Sanctuary Buildings, Great Smith Street, London SW1P 3BT. If you are interested in taking part in an Erasmus or Lingua study period, consult *Erasmus: the UK guide* which lists all institutions taking part in the programmes and details the subjects they offer. This book is available from ISC0, at 12a Princess Way, Camberley, Surrey GU15 3SP, and should be available in careers libraries. For some courses a GCSE or A-level (or the equivalent) in a language will be required; for others students will be taught the relevant language *ab initio* (from scratch).

During, or after, school and college

Study programmes lasting from three weeks to one year are listed below.

Central Bureau for Educational Visits and Exchanges

Central Bureau operates a number of programmes that enable students at school or college to spend time studying in Europe. One of these is described below.

German Courses for Students

This programme is open to young people who have been studying German for at least two years. Students between 16–18 can go to Germany for language tuition and stay with a German family. Courses are arranged every year and students go to Germany during the summer holidays and stay for three weeks. Approximately 40 places are available and students need to apply by April in the year they want to go. Board and lodging are free but students need to pay for their own air fare.

For more information, contact Central Bureau, Seymour Mews, London W1H 9PE (telephone: 0171-486 5101).

Socrates

Under the EU's Socrates programme, the creation of European education projects within schools and colleges will be encouraged. Within these, the mobility of pupils, often to improve language skills, will be supported.

For more information, contact the Department for Education, Sanctuary Buildings, Great Smith Street, London SW1P 3BT.

AFS Intercultural Education Programmes

AFS Intercultural Education Programmes is a non-profit-making voluntary organisation which has been operating since 1946. AFS arranges for 15–18 year olds to spend a year in another country living as a member of a family and going to a local secondary school. Young people in Britain who take part in the programme usually go after GCSEs or A-levels/Advanced GNVQ/BTEC or after Highers or Sixth Year Studies in Scotland.

Before going abroad, young people attend orientation sessions in the UK where discussions take place regarding adapting to life in another country. In the country they go to they will also attend an introductory language course and they will be allocated to a local AFS counsellor who they can contact with any questions or problems.

AFS students can go to a variety of countries in Europe (eg France, Italy, Norway and Slovakia) and further afield (eg Bolivia, Brazil, Chile, Columbia, Honduras, Indonesia, Panama, Paraguay, Thailand, the USA and Venezuela). Each year, AFS in the UK agrees links with certain countries and will then send its students there. The countries available can change each year but, if a student is interested in studying in a particular country, AFS will try to make arrangements to send the young person there.

Those interested in going to Brazil, France, Indonesia,

Italy, Norway, Paraguay, Slovakia, the USA and Venezuela should apply by 31 October to depart the following June/July/August. They will return in June/July after a 12-month programme. Early application is advisable for any country (ie well before the closing date) as the programmes are popular.

It is also possible to do a six-month placement in Bolivia, Chile, Columbia, Honduras, Panama or Thailand. Students should apply to AFS before 31 June and they will leave the UK the next year between January and March and return in July/August. Full-year programmes to these countries can also be arranged and application should be made before 31 October.

Students can benefit in many ways by going on an AFS programme. They will be able to experience a new country and culture and to learn a new language. They will also gain in independence, self-confidence and maturity and will make international friends. For some, it will be the experience of a lifetime.

The cost of going on an AFS programme (1995/6) is £3,950, which includes travel, support, insurance, medical cover, language help, orientation in the UK prior to the visit, accommodation with a family and activities during the year. About £400 spending money will also be needed. AFS does, however, offer financial assistance on a means-tested basis. Over two-thirds of participants ask for, and receive, a financial grant to help pay for the programme costs. Those who are going to apply for financial assistance should do so early as there is a big demand for this help. AFS is keen to make sure that lack of finance is not a factor which prevents young people from taking part in the programme.

Tim Jones

AFS Intercultural Education Programmes case-study

After GCSEs, Tim Jones spent 11 months in Norway via the AFS programme.

‘I found out about AFS from my father who had gone to the United States with AFS in the 1960s. I was keen to take a break after GCSEs and I applied to AFS in January putting the United States, the Caribbean and Norway as my choices of destination.

The selection process involved me, my parents and AFS all filling in a personality form about me. I also had to attend a selection day, which included an interview and various activities that were meant to test leadership, group work, communication and interaction skills.

I was selected by AFS and was given my third choice of country – Norway. Looking back now, I'm glad I went to Norway as I thoroughly enjoyed myself and was able to become fluent in another language. Before I went, I attended a one-day orientation which prepared me for what to expect when I arrived in Norway. After two weeks in Norway, I attended a week's course which helped me with the grammar and language.

I went over to Norway in July and had no knowledge of Norwegian. However, I wasn't apprehensive and just expected to muddle through. In the first two months I mainly spoke English but, after that, I began to understand most of what people were saying. After Christmas, I started to speak Norwegian and, when it was time for me to return to the UK, I was fluent.

I stayed with a family in a small and very quiet village called As, 30 km south of Oslo. The village was in a beautiful area surrounded by forests. Only about 20 people lived there but there were two towns fairly close by.

I generally got on very well with the family although the father irritated me at times (to get me out of bed, he would open the window in the middle of winter letting in the freezing cold!). The family had a son a year older than me who I got on really well with. He'd been to Ecuador via AFS the year before so he knew what I was experiencing.

I attended school but I have to admit that I wasn't very conscientious. I did, though, work quite hard on reading and writing Norwegian and wrote lots of essays.

The school laid on a "Norwegian for foreigners" course two hours a week which helped me with the language.

I found fellow students very friendly and sociable and they were always inviting me back to their homes. I had a very good social life. I made many Norwegian friends and also made friends with other AFS students who I met up with three times during my time in Norway. I now write to people in South America, Australia, New Zealand, Panama and, of course, Norway.

I thoroughly enjoyed all my time in Norway; the highlight was when I went to the Lillehammer Olympics to watch the cross-country skiing. I also went on some skiing holidays where I learnt how to ski downhill and cross-country.

In Norway, there are great seasonal differences with the temperatures falling as low as -25°C in the winter and the summers are long and hot. I saw very little rain in the winter, only snow. I'm keen to return to Norway to work. It's a beautiful country with mountains and forests and does not suffer from the noise, pollution and crime that we accept as part of life in London.

Back in the UK, I am now attending college and I'm taking four A-levels. I have adjusted to living in the UK again and I'm regularly satisfying my craving for junk food! In Norway, people tend to follow a healthy diet of bread, cheese, potatoes and fish. Long-term, I hope to pursue a career which enables me to use my Norwegian.

I would highly recommend AFS to other students. You don't just learn about a new culture and language but you also learn about yourself, tolerance and how you can survive new situations. You are able to see the world from a broader perspective. I think the best time to go is after GCSEs. ’

For more information, contact AFS Intercultural Education Programmes, Ground Floor, Arden House, Wellington Street, Bingley, West Yorkshire BD16 2NB (telephone: 01274 560677, fax: 01274 567675).

AHA (Art History Abroad)

AHA organises spring and summer courses concentrating on art history. It is based in London, Rome, Florence and Venice. The courses generally last for two or six weeks. Accommodation is in hotels; fees include return flight, travel between cities, accommodation, lectures and seminars.

For more information, contact AHA Courses Ltd, Prioryfield House, 20 Canon Street, Taunton, Somerset TA1 1SW (telephone: 01823 323363, fax: 01823 271072).

Challenge Educational Services

Challenge Educational Services organises language programmes at French universities, for post A-level (or equivalent) or degree students, and academic year programmes for those aged 15–18 in schools in Europe (France, Germany and Spain) and the USA.

Course fees for the language programmes in French universities range from £330 to £7,690 (1995) depending on the university attended and the length of time spent in France (courses range from one week to a year). Course fees for the academic year programmes range from £1,760 to £5,590 (1995) depending on the country visited and whether students go for one term/semester or for a year.

For more information and application forms, contact Challenge Educational Services, 101 Lorna Road, Hove, East Sussex BN3 3EL (telephone: 01273 220261).

Council on International Educational Exchange (CIEE)

CIEE is a non-profit-making organisation that exists to further international education. It offers opportunities to study abroad at universities worldwide for a summer, semester or academic year. In Europe, summer language courses are offered in France and study abroad programmes lasting from three to 56 weeks are offered in several countries including Belgium, Czech Republic, France, Germany, Hungary, The Netherlands, Poland, Spain and Russia. Programmes are open to gap–year students, undergraduates, postgraduates and young professionals. For gap-year students, specific programmes in Europe are offered in Belgium, the Czech Republic, France, Hungary, The Netherlands, Poland and Spain. Programmes are of a very high quality and offer US university credit. Deadlines are at various points in the year, but applicants should contact CIEE no later than the start of their last year at school to have a full choice of courses. Fees apply to all programmes, but for students who are keen CIEE can offer assistance with fundraising activities.

For further details, contact Council on International Educational Exchange, 33 Seymour Place, London W1H 6AT (telephone: 0171-706 3008, fax: 0171-724 8468).

European Business Management School

The European Business Management School organises a one-year European Business Preparation Course which combines business studies, French, German or Spanish, projects, practical and personal skills, study visits and work experience with periods in London and either Paris, Munich or Madrid. The course is designed with a practical and vocational emphasis for students who have completed A-levels, GNVQs, BTECs (or equivalent). Students will gain an insight into business and management, develop a foreign business language and discover another country's culture. They will learn research, analytical and presentation techniques and will acquire business, interpersonal skills and confidence.

The course is particularly suitable for students who are looking for a constructive way to spend a gap year, who wish to gain business knowledge and business-related work experience, who want to improve a language and work/study abroad and who want to strengthen their personal and social skills before going on to university or into employment. Students mix with over 220 other European students on a range of different courses and teaching is conducted in small groups by experienced lecturers.

The tuition fees for the one-year course in 1994/5 are £2,600 plus a £100 registration fee payable on acceptance of a definite place. Additional funds to cover living expenses, rent and travel will be needed by the student. EBMS can help students find accommodation.

For more information, contact The Registrar, EBMS, 64–78 Kingsway, London WC2B 6AH (telephone: 0171-405 6800).

Language and other courses

The organisations listed below run language and other courses in continental Europe. For details of other organisations that run courses in the UK and in continental Europe, see chapter 10.

Cultural and Educational Services Abroad

Contact this organisation for details of language courses abroad. Write to Western House, Malpas, Truro, Cornwall TR1 1SQ (telephone: 01872 225300).

EF International Language Schools

EF runs language courses abroad, both short-term and up to an academic year. For more information, contact EF International Language Schools, 74 Roupell Street, London SE1 8SS (Telephone: 0171-401 3660).

Euro-Academy

For more information on language courses abroad, contact Euro-Academy, 77a George Street, Croydon, Surrey CR0 1LD (telephone: 0181-686 2363/681 2905).

Experiment in International Living

This organisation runs language courses in Europe and worldwide. For further details see its entry in the following section on paying guests, homestays and exchange visits.

Experiment Séjours Educatifs Internationaux

This French organisation runs short- and long-term (year long) language programmes in institutions and universities in France. For more details and prices, contact Experiment Séjours Educatifs Internationaux, 89 rue de Turbigo, 75003 Paris, France (telephone: 00 33 1 42 78 50 03).

John Hall Pre-University Interim Course

John Hall offers courses in Italy on European civilisation, especially the visual arts and music, for non-specialists. They include practical options such as languages, drawing, painting and photography. There is a spring course in Venice costing £3,300 with optional extra periods in Florence and Rome.

For more information, contact the Secretary, John Hall Pre-University Course, 12 Gainsborough Road, Ipswich, Suffolk IP4 2UR (telephone: 01473 251223).

Exchange programmes

The following organisation is one of several that arranges exchange programmes in continental Europe.

Youth for Understanding (YFU)

YFU is a private, non-profit-making, long-established international educational exchange organisation. It started in the USA in 1951 and aims to promote international understanding and world peace. Now, more than 37 countries are involved. YFU's core programme is an educational exchange experience. Each year, it operates approximately 190 programmes and about 8,000 students from around the world participate in them.

YFU encourages parents to become involved by being host parents and encourages students to widen their horizons as exchange students experiencing the everyday life, language and culture in their chosen country. YFU also provides further opportunities for students, when they return, to participate in training in Europe and to attend international seminars. Exchange students from the UK can go to the USA or a European country for a year, live with a (carefully selected) host family and attend school there. Alternatively, they can choose to go to Japan for six months. From January 1996, British students will also be able to go to New Zealand, and from January 1997 to Australia, for six months. Students who choose a European country, or Japan, will spend time learning the language and may come back able to speak it fluently. Students attend a residential weekend of training before they leave and there is also further training in the host country. YFU also provides caring support to students throughout the year.

The exchange programme is open to young people aged 16–18 who want to experience a new culture and gain maturity and language ability. The costs of the programmes are: USA £3,750, Europe £2,750, Japan £4,000. Programme fees for participants include the selection, orientation, insurance, travel and support/counselling in the receiving country. YFU gives advice and help to students regarding raising this fee. Early application is advisable. In addition, YFU UK operates in partnership with education departments in countries worldwide to provide culture awareness social education packages.

If you are living in the UK, you should contact YFU UK, YFU Office, Unit 1 D 3, Templeton Business Centre, 62 Templeton Street, Glasgow G40 1DA (telephone: 0141-556 1116, fax: 0141-551 0949) for more information.

Paying guests, homestays and exchange visits

Being a paying guest enables you to spend time in a foreign country and to learn the language and about the culture while living as part of a family. It can also be combined with study. The cost of accommodation and the length of visits vary; for full details contact the organisations mentioned below.

A home-to-home exchange is a cheaper way of taking part in the life of a family abroad and allows you to return their hospitality. Some of the agencies mentioned can arrange these visits. *Home from Home,* published by Central Bureau, also gives details of exchanges and paying guest visits.

In the au pair section in Part 3, you will find details on the following organisations which can also arrange paying guest or homestay visits abroad – Accueil Familial des Jeunes Etrangers, Inter-Séjours, Jolaine Au Pair Agency and ÖKISTA.

Exchange visits are normally between two young people of a similar age who are still in education. They usually spend two weeks or more in each other's homes. Accommodation and food in the host country are usually free and the family often organises trips to see places of interest. Central Bureau for Educational Visits and Exchanges can put schools and colleges in touch with partners abroad for the purpose of exchanges and also operates a penfriend service for young people between the ages of 8–18. Penfriends may then want to organise their own exchange.

Central Bureau can be contacted at Seymour Mews, London W1H 9PE (telephone: 0171-486 5101).

Anglo-Austrian Society

Besides specialising in travel to Austria, the Anglo-Austrian Society also offers German language courses in England and Austria for young people aged 15 and over, as well as school holiday exchanges, when pupils stay with Austrian families, and youth group travel.

For more information, contact the Anglo-Austrian Society, 46 Queen Anne's Gate, London SW1H 9AU (telephone: 0171-222 0366).

Atlantis Youth Exchange

Atlantis Youth Exchange is a Norwegian organisation which offers au pair programmes for Norwegians in a number of countries including the USA and all western European countries. It also arranges for young people from other European countries, including the UK, to work as au pairs in Norway. In the language field, it runs courses in all major languages. It also arranges short-term agricultural programmes for foreigners in Norway. Other areas in which it is involved include a short-term working guest programme, where young people live and work within a Norwegian family, usually on a farm, and the 'Youth for Europe' programme. It can give advice on the organisation and finance of youth exchanges.

For more information, contact Atlantis Youth

Exchange, Rolf Hofmosgate 18, 0655 Oslo, Norway (telephone: 00 47 22 670043, fax: 00 47 22 686808).

En Famille Overseas

En Famille Overseas arranges paying guest visits in several European countries and language courses in France.

For more information, contact En Famille Overseas, Old Stables, 60b Maltravers Street, Arundel, East Sussex BN8 9BG (telephone: 01903 883266).

Euroyouth

Euroyouth works in co-operation with a number of continental youth travel organisations and with schools and colleges. As well as running programmes in the UK for young people from overseas, it also sends UK people to a number of European countries which include Austria, Belgium, France, Greece, Italy, The Netherlands, Portugal and Spain. It can arrange for students to stay with families in Europe either as holiday guests or paying guests. Holiday guests undertake to make English conversation with the hosts and their children for about 3–4 hours daily. Paying guests go to speak the language of the host country and pay the family for their stay.

For more information, contact Euroyouth, 301 Westborough Road, Westcliff, Southend-on-Sea, Essex SS0 9PT (telephone: 01702 341434).

Experiment in International Living (EIL)

Experiment in International Living (EIL) is a non-profit-making educational travel organisation founded in 1932 in the USA. The first programme involved a group of Americans spending a summer 'experiment' living in Switzerland and Germany; hence the name.

The aims of EIL are to promote greater peace, understanding and friendship between people in different parts of the world. This aim is largely achieved by arranging for participants to spend a period (known as a 'homestay') living in the home of a host in one of many countries around the world. Some of EIL's programmes are linked with language courses and study overseas. For example, it is possible to study French in France while living with a

French family. Other programmes are presented as a 'more exciting and adventurous alternative' to a package holiday. EIL programmes typically last for a period of between one and four weeks.

A fee is charged for participation in all EIL programmes. For example, a four-week homestay in France costs approximately £500. This fee covers accommodation costs and the services of a local EIL representative. However, the costs of travel and insurance are not included and these must be arranged and paid for by the participant. EIL can, though, help with sponsorship for homestay programmes.

EIL host families are specially selected for their willingness to welcome foreigners into their homes and share their way of life. Participants must be friendly and flexible and prepared to adapt to conditions locally, which in many places are more basic than those at home. The age range for participants is 16–70.

EIL operates an au pair programme in Europe and in the USA (Au Pair Homestay USA). It also organises university and college placements in the USA.

Further details on all EIL programmes can be obtained from EIL Limited, Otesaga, West Malvern Road, Malvern, Worcestershire WR14 4EN (telephone: 01684 562577).

Experiment Séjours Educatifs Internationaux

This French organisation arranges individual homestays from 1–4 weeks with French families. For more details, contact Experiment Séjours Educatifs Internationaux, 89 rue de Turbigo, 75003 Paris, France (telephone: 00 33 1 42 78 50 03).

Host and Guest Service

This organisation arranges stays for paying guests in France and other European countries. For further information, contact Carol Rutter, Host and Guest Service, Harwood House, 27 Effie Road, London SW6 1EN (telephone: 0171-731 5340).

15 Travel in Continental Europe

During some of your time out, you may want to travel around Europe experiencing the different cultures, learning about the history, meeting fellow Europeans and generally having a good time. Below, you will find some useful information to digest before you go, some of which will be helpful whatever you decide to do.

ISIC card

Travel abroad can be expensive, but all people over the age of 12, who are in full-time education, are eligible for an International Student Identity Card (ISIC). The ISIC is the only document that is internationally accepted as proof of your student status and it entitles holders to reductions on travel fares and on charges to places of interest in the UK and abroad. ISIC cards cost £5 and applicants also receive a free copy of the *ISIC World Travel Handbook*. There is also an ISIC Helpline, a special emergency service, which can be used from anywhere in the world. An application for an ISIC card must be accompanied by:

1. Valid proof of full-time student status (eg a letter from your school/college/university with an official stamp or a National Union of Students (NUS) membership card)
2. A passport photograph.

ISIC cards are obtainable from student travel offices/ unions or by post from ISIC Mail Order, Bleaklow House, Howard Town Mills, Mill Street, Glossop, Derbyshire SK13 8PT.

Getting there

How you choose to travel will obviously depend on your budget and the time you have available. Don't forget, though, that sometimes the best part about a trip is getting there.

By train

British Rail offers two main cheap rail passes for the under-26s. These include the Inter-Rail Pass and the Freedom Pass.

With the **Inter-Rail Pass** it is possible to travel around Europe for a month for £249 (1995 price). If you only want to go to a few countries it is possible to buy a cheaper ticket for just two or three zones; for a month the cheapest ticket is £209. You can also buy a 15-day ticket to travel in one zone for £179.

The zones are:

1 Republic of Ireland
2 Finland, Norway, Sweden
3 Austria, Denmark, Germany, Switzerland
4 Bulgaria, Croatia, Czech Republic, Hungary, Poland, Romania, Slovakia
5 Belgium, France, Luxembourg, The Netherlands
6 Morocco, Portugal, Spain
7 Greece, Italy, Slovenia, Turkey.

The **Freedom Pass** is a ticket that enables you to ride the length and breadth of the national rail network in the European country of your choice for a very cheap price. Passes offer travel on any three, five or ten days within a one-month period so that you can visit any one of the 26 European countries in your own time. For those under 26, prices range from £11 for three days in Luxembourg to £204 (1995 prices) for ten days in France.

Over 26?

Passes are also available for those over 26. An Inter-Rail Pass for 15 days costs £209 and for one month costs £269. Freedom Passes are also available; a second-class ticket for three days in Luxembourg costs £16 and the most expensive second class ten-day ticket, in France, costs £239. The prices quoted above were correct for 1995.

For further information, contact the International Rail Centre, Victoria Station, London SW1Y 1JY (telephone: 0171-834 2345).

By plane

STA Travel and Campus Travel offer discounted flights for students and young people under 26. Both will issue students with an ISIC card if they can produce evidence of being in full-time education.

By coach

This can be the cheapest way of travelling if you can cope with overnight trips and snatched moments of sleep. National Express Coaches have a discount card for full-time students or young people under 25. The card costs £7 and entitles you to a third off bus trips in the UK and many European cities. National Express Coaches can be contacted on 0171-730 0202 or write to National Express Coaches, Victoria Coach Station, Buckingham Palace Road, London SW1V 1JU.

Student travel agencies

The Council on International Educational Exchange operates a travel agency called Council Travel which specialises in offering a travel service to students and under-26 year olds. It deals with European and worldwide destinations and can arrange coach, train or air travel plus travel insurance. For more details, contact Council Travel at 28a Poland Street, London W1V 3DB (telephone: European sales 0171-287 3337, worldwide sales 0171-437 7767).

STA Travel, which has offices in major UK cities, offers discounted travel to students and those under 26.

Campus Travel, based at 36 locations throughout the UK (and many bases on university campuses), is a big supplier of student/youth travel to the UK student market. It deals with every method of travel and offers flexible tickets, which means that dates and destinations can be changed and money can be refunded.

Accommodation

You are likely to be on a fairly tight budget. Fortunately, there are excellent inexpensive, clean and safe places for young people to stay throughout Europe.

Youth Hostelling

If you are planning to travel around Europe, it would be worthwhile joining the Youth Hostel Association (YHA). YHA membership opens the door to 5,000 youth hostels in 60 countries. Youth hostels are usually much cheaper than other accommodation available. If you buy an Inter-Rail Pass you may be able to join the YHA for a discounted price. The YHA produces handbooks of youth hostels throughout the world.

For more information, contact the YHA, 8 St Stephen's Hill, St Albans, Hertfordshire AL1 2DY (telephone: 01727 855215).

YMCA (Young Men's Christian Association)

There are YMCA hostels throughout the world that offer cheap accommodation and welcome both women and men (it is not necessary to be a Christian to stay in them). The National Council of YMCAs is based at 640 Forest Road, London E17 3DZ (telephone: 0181-520 5599). You can order the YMCA's *World Directory* for £4 from the National Council. This gives information on YMCAs worldwide.

Useful guides

The Lonely Planet series of guides to many countries and areas of the world provides excellent information on budget accommodation as well as giving information on travel, sightseeing and potential problems and hazards to be aware of. The series is available in most major bookshops.

Other guides you will find useful include the Rough Guide series, the Let's Go budget series, the Berkeley Guide series, the Blue Guide series and Fodor's travel guides. Most of these series cover individual countries and some include individual city guides.

Insurance

Make sure that you organise comprehensive travel insurance before you go which covers medical fees and loss of personal belongings. Also, remember to complete the certificate of entitlement to reciprocal healthcare in the European Union (E111), available from post offices, before you leave the UK (see chapter 11 for more details).

ISIS (International Student Insurance Service) provides reasonably priced insurance cover for young people. Details of ISIS are given in chapter 11.

Inoculations

For most European countries inoculations will not be needed. However, for some countries, particularly the hotter ones, inoculations may be recommended so check this with your GP about a month before you plan to go travelling.

Finance

Make sure that you have enough money to cover all eventualities (including illness and accidents). Many people decide to take traveller's cheques. These are a good idea particularly if you will be travelling in areas where there is a high crime rate and where pickpocketing is rife. If you keep details of all your traveller's cheques they can be replaced if they are stolen. A Visa or Access card can be useful if you get into financial difficulties. To avoid this, though, try to calculate how much you're likely to spend by finding out approximate costs of travel and accommodation and by researching the costs of living in the countries you intend to travel to.

For more detailed information on what to think about before travelling abroad, see chapter 20.

National tourist offices in London can also be a very good source of information about the countries they represent. See the Country Index in Part 5 for details of some of the tourist offices representing European countries.

4

Taking Time Out Worldwide

16 Paid Employment Worldwide

If you want to work in the rest of the world, there are many opportunities open to you. These include a working holiday in Australia, au pairing in the Canary Islands, working on a children's camp in America, teaching English in the Far East or working on a farm in New Zealand. Alternatively, you might want to organise a relevant placement abroad during your degree course. You will probably find it helpful to read Part 3 on Europe since many organisations offering opportunities in Europe also operate worldwide.

Work permits

If you intend to find your own work in a country outside the European Union, you will need to get a work permit. Sometimes these are difficult to acquire, since a number of countries restrict the numbers of people entering their country for work purposes. This is often due to the fact that their levels of unemployment are high and jobs are hard to find. They also want to protect jobs for their own nationals. If you have a skill for which there is a demand in the country you wish to visit, then you may find it easier to get a work permit. For information on work permits and entry regulations, contact the embassy representing the country you want to go to in London. You will find details of these in Part 5. Sometimes you can get caught in the 'you can't get a work permit unless you have a job' dilemma. You will also need to check the employment/unemployment situation before you go.

On a more positive note, though, there are many organisations that specifically recruit UK people for jobs overseas. The US government strictly restricts the issue of work permits (if you're Irish, your chances of getting one are greater) but it does support many organisations that run approved exchanges and international cultural exchanges, such as Camp America, BUNAC and au pair agencies, which offer opportunities for Europeans to work in America from a few months up to a year. The American embassy visa branch is based at 5 Upper Grosvenor Street, London W1A 2JB. *Summer Jobs USA* published by Vacation Work is worth consulting if America is your first choice.

Jobs in newspapers

When looking for a job from this country, you could consult the newspaper *Overseas Jobs Express* (to subscribe, contact *Overseas Jobs Express*, PO Box 22, Brighton, East Sussex BN1 6HX) or the magazine *Jobs International* (available from Cromwell Court, New Road, St Ives, Cambridgeshire PE17 4BG). Both include advertisements of short-term and long-term jobs overseas. You could also ask about overseas vacancies in your local Jobcentre. You may find, though, that many jobs you see advertised require skills and experience.

In the following sections, you will find details of organisations, many with a base in the UK, that can organise work for you in other parts of the world. You may find the prospect of going with a reputable organisation less daunting.

Working holidays

A working holiday in Australia or New Zealand attracts many people. Young people aged 18–25 can apply for an Australian working holiday visa. They need to show evidence of £2,000 in their bank account to support themselves on their trip and to pay for their air fare. They can undertake casual work in Australia with each job lasting no more than three months. Applicants between 26–30 will also be considered if they can prove that their trip will benefit themselves and Australia.

For more information, contact the Australian embassy in London (for address see Part 5).

Currently, the New Zealand embassy administers a scheme whereby 500 people from the UK aged between 18–30 can visit New Zealand and undertake temporary casual work. Applicants need the equivalent of NZ$4,200 to pay for their trip and return flight.

For more details, contact the New Zealand embassy in London (for address see Part 5).

There is no working holiday scheme in Canada and the issue of a work permit is usually dependent on the applicant finding a job and then the employer requests the permit. However, university students, who find a job for the summer or for their sandwich year, can apply for visas.

For more information, contact the Canadian embassy immigration visa section, 38 Grosvenor Street, London W1X 0AA.

BUNAC (see below) does have a work placement scheme in Canada (see section on work placements later in this chapter).

British Universities North America Club (BUNAC)

BUNAC organises a number of working holiday programmes in Australia for students and young people.

Work Australia

Work Australia offers young people aged 18–25 (inclusive) the chance to live and work in Australia for up to one year. The programme features a round-trip flight, working holiday visa, Hawaii stop-over (if flying from Los Angeles), ongoing support and assistance, mail forwarding, orientations and two nights' accommodation in Sydney. Applicants must be citizens of the UK, Canada, the Republic of Ireland or The Netherlands. In 1994, fees for this programme, for participants flying from the UK, ranged from £1,295 to £1,455.

Working as an au pair or nanny

There are many agencies that can arrange for you to work as an au pair in America and Canada and even the

Canary Islands. A number of these agencies have already been mentioned in chapter 11 in Part 3, so please refer to this for more details. The agencies already referred to in Part 3 are Aaron Employment Agency (Canada), Avalon Agency (USA), Galentinas (USA), Helping Hands Agency (Canada) and Inter-Séjours (Canary Islands).

There are a number of agencies that specialise in sending au pairs to America and have the full support of the US government. The conditions, which changed in February 1995, are generally the same for all. Applicants should usually be between 18–26 and have childcare experience (eg babysitting) or a childcare qualification (eg NNEB, BTEC) and a full driving licence. Prior to departure, each applicant *must* show that they have received eight hours of child safety training, ie a first aid certificate from the British Red Cross or St John Ambulance. Applicants may be asked to provide a returnable good faith deposit of £300 to ensure their commitment. Au pairs work for 12 months looking after children and often also doing light housework. Au pairs are given a year's visa and receive $115–$150 (depending on qualifications) per week, return flight paid for, medical insurance, $500 towards a course, board and lodging in the family home, two weeks' paid holiday and a month at the end to travel around America. They are encouraged to meet and make friends with other au pairs in their area and usually attend an orientation session on arrival in America. They also have the support of a local counsellor during their stay. Below, you will find the details of organisations offering these au pair opportunities and will be able to read about one girl's experience as an au pair in America.

Au Pair Care

This agency places au pairs in America with the full support of the US authorities. A 12-month scheme is open to people aged 18–26 with a driver's licence and some childcare experience. Visa, return flight, medical insurance,

$115–$150 per week pocket money (depending on qualifications), full board and lodging, a two-week paid vacation and the full support of a local counsellor during your stay are all provided. Au pairs attend monthly meetings and quarterly seminars with the local US counsellor.

For further information and an application form, contact the Programme Manager, Au Pair Care, 101 Lorna Road, Hove, East Sussex BN3 3EL (telephone: 01273 220261).

Au Pair/Homestay USA

The Au Pair/Homestay USA programme offers people aged 18–26 the opportunity to live in the United States for a year, working 45 hours per week providing childcare for a host family. Programme participants receive a round-trip air fare, full room and board with their host family, a $115–$150 per week stipend (depending on qualifications), a year-long visa, a $500 education subsidy from the host family, the possibility of doing an educational or professional internship, two weeks' paid vacation, full insurance, support via the local programme staff and have consistent contact with other European au pairs participating in the programme. There is also an optional month, after the programme, to tour the country.

For more information, contact Experiment in International Living, Otesaga, West Malvern Road, Malvern, Worcestershire WR14 4EN (telephone: 01684 562577).

Au Pair in America

This agency places au pairs in America for a period of 12 months. Pocket money of $115–$150 per week (depending on qualifications) is guaranteed with two weeks off with pocket money during placement. The host family also provides $500 for the au pair to take an educational course. Au Pair in America provides return travel to the host family and arranges a visa and medical insurance; applicants must place a deposit which is refunded after completion of the placement. A four-day orientation/

training session is run upon arrival in New York. Applicants must be aged 18–26, have some experience of childcare (eg babysitting) and hold a full driving licence. Au Pair in America has interviewers throughout the UK and au pairs leave for the USA every month.

Michaela Wiggins

Au Pair in America case-study

Michaela was feeling a bit disillusioned with her life and her work as a hairdresser when she visited some relatives in West Virginia. Once in the USA, she was inspired to look into opportunities to spend time working there. She got hold of *How To Live and Work in America* (see Reading List in Part 5 for details) and found out about Au Pair in America. She decided to apply and was invited for an interview.

‘The interview was very relaxed. They asked me about my previous experience with children and the only experience required was babysitting. I got through the interview and they asked me to organise character references from a previous employer and a family friend. They also checked my medical records. This was all fine and I was accepted. My application form was then circulated to families in America.

Families who are interested in your application will telephone you and interview you over the phone. I didn't feel happy with the first family who phoned but the second family seemed a lot more friendly. I talked to them for nearly two hours. They asked me about my childcare experience, what I would do in certain situations and what activities I would organise for the children. I felt that I would get on well with this family so I accepted their offer.

I spent four days in New York on an orientation course with about 150 other au pairs from all over Europe. We stayed in a hotel near Central Park and we were told about American culture and what to expect. We had a talk from a recent au pair who told us about her experiences. We also learnt about first aid. Most of the au pairs had just left home for the first time. Evenings were free and I managed to see all the famous sights.

On the fourth day, I flew to the host family in Cleveland, Ohio. They met me at the airport. My job was to look after four children aged between two and ten years. To begin with, it was a bit daunting and I found it hard adjusting to living with the family.

In the first two weeks, the children's mother was around quite a bit and this helped me to get used to the new situation gradually. I soon got my own routine. I helped the children with drawing and Lego, organised play activities and took them for walks. Au Pair in America put me in touch with other au pairs in my area and I often went around to see them with the children. I made friends with lots of other au pairs and we all compared notes on the best places to go out.

It wasn't always rosy with the family, though. I had to talk to the parents about discipline and set down some ground rules. I am naturally shy but I learnt that you have to speak up for yourself and discuss issues openly. The four year old was also quite difficult to begin with as he had become very attached to the previous au pair. Au pair work isn't glamorous and it can be hard work looking after children; sometimes you crave adult conversation. However, the work is very rewarding and I can claim as my successes potty training a two year old and teaching a four year old to read and write. It was enjoyable seeing the children developing and noticing the effect I was having on their lives. To be a successful au pair, I think you just need to be mature and have common sense.

I had a fantastic year in America. I made some great friends and had a good social life, learnt Spanish and developed a very good relationship with my host family. I also managed to see quite a bit of America. As well as New York, I went to Washington DC, West Virginia and

Florida. The year abroad made me more independent and outgoing.

I'm back home now, working in London as a nanny. In the first few months, I found it difficult adjusting to life in the UK. I would love to go back to America to live there permanently but getting a visa is difficult.

I would wholeheartedly recommend au pair work in America. You are only young once and you should take advantage of opportunities; it broadens your horizons and you have a great year. My experience as an au pair in America totally changed my life – for the better. Not only did it make me more confident, but living in a different culture made me more tolerant of new people, ideas and situations. And I'm 100 per cent happier with my life now than before I went. ❜

For more information, contact Au Pair in America, 37 Queen's Gate, London SW7 5HR (telephone: 0171-581 7322/direct 7357). Please call freephone 0800 413116 for a brochure and an application form.

Canary Islands Bureau

Au pairs (girls only) wanted for the Canary Islands for 4–12 months. Duties include housework and childcare, occasionally with language tuition. Au pairs are free for three hours daily and one day and two evenings weekly. Applications, in writing only, must be accompanied by photograph, references and international reply coupon.

For more information, contact Canary Islands Bureau, Urb. Santiago, B 4-5e dcha, 38005 Santa Cruz de Tenerife.

Childcare America

Visa-supported one-year stays in the USA are arranged for applicants aged 18–26 years. Childcare experience is required; drivers and non-smokers are preferred. Applicants can choose their host family and they will have the opportunity to attend a part-time college course. Support is available from a local counsellor. Return air fare and medical insurance is paid plus two weeks' vacation. Applicants can start at any time and can earn $115–$150 per week, depending on qualifications.

For more information, contact Childcare International Ltd, Trafalgar House, Grenville Place, London NW7 3SA (telephone: 0181-959 3611/906 3116, fax: 0181-906 3461).

Childcare Canada

Childcare International arranges live-in family placements in Canada for those with a nanny/teaching/nursing qualification. The minimum stay is one year and applicants must be over 18. Support and assistance are given throughout the stay.

For more information, contact Childcare International Ltd, Trafalgar House, Grenville Place, London NW7 3SA (telephone: 0181-959 3611/906 3116, fax: 0181-906 3461).

EF Au Pair

EF Au Pair offers the opportunity to work in the USA for one year for 18–26 year olds. Au pairs share the life of an American family and have the chance to study and explore the USA. Working conditions as an EF Au Pair are carefully controlled. The host family is carefully chosen and au pairs have the support of a personal counsellor. They are provided with free flights, insurance, an official visa, $115–$150 per week (depending on qualifications), $500 contribution towards their studies, two weeks' paid holiday and a bonus 13th month for travel. The maximum hours of work are 45 hours a week over five-and-a-half days. Applicants should have some childcare experience and be able to drive. It is advisable to apply 3–4 months before you want to leave and there are monthly departures to America.

For more information, contact EF Au Pair, 74 Roupell Street, London SE1 8SS (telephone: 0171-401 8004).

Students Abroad Limited

This organisation, which specialises in placing au pairs in Europe, also arranges placements for au pairs with host families in the USA. To join the USA programme, you must be aged 18–26, have some childcare experience, have a full driving licence and be a non-smoker. Posts are available throughout the USA for one year. Flights and medical insurance are paid and applicants have the opportunity to attend a college course of their choice. Benefits include two weeks' vacation, a 24-hour local counsellor and $115–$150 per week pocket money (depending on qualifications) for up to 45 hours' work.

All applicants are required to complete a registration form, which should be returned with eight photographs, two references, a clean medical certificate and an introduction letter to the prospective host family.

For information and a registration form, please send a large SAE to Students Abroad Ltd, 11 Milton View, Hitchin, Hertfordshire SG4 0QD (telephone: 01462 438909).

Working on children's camps

In the next section, you will find details about working on children's camps in America. BUNAC, Camp America and Camp Counselors USA are the main organisations that recruit for these camps and they look for children's counsellors as well as other staff to work in catering, laundry, maintenance and office areas.

British Universities North America Club (BUNAC)

BUNAC organises a number of work exchange programmes between the USA, Canada and the UK for students and young people.

BUNACAMP

BUNACAMP requires students, and non-students, between the ages of 19 and a half (by July) and 35 to work as camp counsellors on children's summer camps in America from June to mid/end August. Working as a counsellor may mean teaching or supervising an activity or acting as a confidential adviser to the children. A registration fee of £59 is required. BUNACAMP finds placements for suitable applicants, arranges return flights, visa and insurance. Camps provide board and lodging and a salary of $390–$450. Applicants must be energetic and hard-working, and have some previous experience of working with groups of children.

WAP/KAMP

Work America Programme (WAP) and Kitchen and Maintenance Programme (KAMP) offer students studying full-time at HND or degree level (or, for the KAMP programme, an appropriate level catering course) the chance to work in a variety of jobs during the summer months (June–September). Students in their gap year, who are at least 18, and who have an unconditional higher education place for the following autumn, can also apply. WAP entitles you to take any job in the USA and KAMP entitles you to do a variety of non-counselling jobs on summer camps. The registration fee for the WAP programme is £81. Participants pay for their own flight and insurance. It costs £69 to register for the KAMP programme and participants also pay for their own insurance.

Sally Butterworth

BUNAC and Work Australia case-study

Sally, 23, is in the first year of a degree in biology and applied computing information systems at Roehampton Institute. She spent three summers on children's camps in America working as a secretary and live-in counsellor organising social activities for BUNAC staff. By her third summer, she was given more responsibility and was involved in showing visitors around the camp.

‘I got my first job with BUNAC as a secretary because I had worked as a medical secretary in the UK. I really enjoyed the work and the social life on the camp and I made lots of friends from all over the world. Food and accommodation was provided and I got paid between $390–$450 for eight/nine weeks' work. After each camp, I travelled around America and Canada.

After the second time on the camp, I went on

BUNAC's Work Australia programme*. They organise flights, visas, two nights' accommodation and orientation when you arrive in Sydney and provide back-up help in Australia. They also arrange for those on the programme to spend a week getting to know each other in Hawaii so that no one is alone on arrival in Australia.

I met up with a group of 16 other BUNAC students and nine of us shared a flat for three months near Bondi. Six girls shared one room and three guys the other. It was a bit cramped but we were out a lot and it meant we only paid £17 a week each for rent.

I didn't find it difficult getting temping jobs and used Manpower and Templine agencies. I had good secretarial skills and office work was fairly easy to find. I was able to save quite a lot of money, mainly because of my cheap rent, and I spent the money travelling around Australia. I travelled by campervan up the east coast with some friends from home. We stopped at Magnetic and Fraser Islands and learnt to scuba dive off Cairns.

After my friends went home, I travelled alone to Melbourne and Adelaide. You meet a lot of people if you're on your own. I also went on a double-decker bus adventure tour in Perth, Western Australia. Lots of activities were arranged such as caving, swimming, dolphin-watching and fruit-picking. The trip was great fun.

I returned to Sydney and travelled home via Hong Kong and Thailand. In Thailand, I trekked amongst the hill tribes on foot, by bamboo raft and on the back of an elephant. It was great.

The Work Australia programme is really good for the first-time traveller because BUNAC provides back-up and security. Young people travelling around the world should be careful. My advice would be keep your wits about you, don't be too trusting of people, don't hitch-hike alone but also don't be put off doing things you're keen to do. I've now got the travel bug badly and my next stop is Kenya. ’

* see section on working holidays

BUNAC programmes are popular so it is essential to apply early. For more details on any of the programmes mentioned above, contact BUNAC, 16 Bowling Green Lane, London EC1R 0BD (telephone: 0171-251 3472, fax: 0171-251 0215).

Camp America

Camp America arranges for young people (18–35) to work on US summer camps for ten weeks either as counsellors (looking after children) or as camp power workers (working in the kitchen, laundry, office, etc). There are also places for applicants who wish to look after children in American families for ten weeks. Camp America offers free return flight, board and lodging, pocket money and up to six weeks for independent travel.

Apply before the end of April in the year you wish to participate. Applicants must be available from 30 June. Approximately 6,600 people are recruited annually.

For more information, contact Department AYO, 37a Queen's Gate, London SW7 5HR (telephone: 0171-581 7373).

Camp Counselors USA Ltd

Camp Counselors USA places young people, who are aged 18–30, in jobs at US summer camps where they work for nine weeks from June through to August. When the camp assignment ends, participants are free to travel independently for up to ten weeks before they return home or continue travelling elsewhere.

Camp Counselors USA is looking for people who wish to work with children as counsellors, or students who are interested in its support staff programme. Support staff work in the kitchen or laundry, in the office or doing maintenance work. Applicants for camp counsellor positions must have had experience of working with children and those who are able to teach or lead activities in areas such as science and nature, arts and crafts, sports, outdoor skills, watersports and performing arts are at an advantage. However, enthusiasm and a positive attitude are also valuable attributes.

Applicants pay a deposit of £45 (£20 before 31 January) and £135 insurance. They receive a designated amount of money for the nine weeks on the camp which ranges from $300 to $650. Those who work for more than nine weeks, receive $105–$140 for every extra week worked. Returning counsellors pay only £70 to go back to camp, which includes deposit and insurance. Camp Counselors USA pays for the return flight, transportation to the camp and organises the visa and the orientation session. Accommodation is provided on the camp.

Camp Counselors USA can also help students looking for placements in the leisure and catering industries in the USA.

For more information, contact Camp Counselors USA, 154a Heath Road, Twickenham, London TW1 4BN (telephone: 0181-744 9060) or, if you live in Scotland, 27 Woodside Gardens, Musselburgh, Lothian EH21 7LJ (telephone: 0131-665 5843).

Working in the tourist industry

If you want to work in the travel and tourism industry, you could consider working in hotels or as a courier or overseas representative. Opportunities in these areas are covered in chapter 11 in Part 3.

Teaching English as a foreign language

If you have a TEFL qualification, such as the RSA Preparatory Certificate, and preferably a degree, you will have a good chance of finding a job teaching English abroad. TEFL is covered in some detail in chapter 10. You will find details on qualifications available, and the addresses of language schools in the UK that recruit teachers for summer courses if you want to gain some experience in the UK before going abroad. Part 3 gives details of where to look for jobs and the details of agencies in the UK that recruit teachers.

Central Bureau for Educational Visits and Exchanges

Central Bureau recruits English language assistants to teach in Latin America for a year. For further details of their English Language Assistants Programme, see pages 110–111.

Louise Pole-Baker

Language assistant case-study

During her humanities degree course Louise Pole-Baker spent a year in Columbia as a language assistant.

‘Competition for language assistant places in South America is fierce and usually an A-level in Spanish is required. With just an O-level in Spanish from ten years ago, I wasn't sure if I'd stand a chance. However, I was very keen to go and eventually I was accepted.

I started teaching children aged from seven to nine, which was a nightmare. I couldn't speak much Spanish, the children couldn't speak any English so discipline was impossible. I then moved on to teaching classes at a private language school. After a few months, when I had picked up more Spanish, I found keeping discipline easier and, by the end of the year, I was thoroughly enjoying teaching.

I learnt a great deal: my spoken Spanish improved dramatically, I learnt how to teach, I became more assertive and I got to travel around a stunning country.’

Council on International Educational Exchange (CIEE)

The Council on International Educational Exchange recruits graduates for a teaching English programme in Japan called the Japanese Exchange and Teaching (JET) Programme. CIEE recruit 350–400 graduates of any subject for assistant language teacher (and co-ordinator for international relations) positions on behalf of the

Japanese government. Contracts are for a minimum of a year. Help is given with finding accommodation, flights are paid for and pay is approximately £22,000 per annum.

For more information, contact CIEE, 33 Seymour Place, London W1H 6AT (telephone: 0171-224 8896).

Work placements

If you want to take up a work placement abroad during your degree course, you should look into opportunities through AIESEC and IAESTE. These programmes cover approximately 81 and 64 countries worldwide respectively. You will find full details of their programmes in chapter 11 in Part 3.

British Universities North America Club (BUNAC)

BUNAC organises a number of work placement programmes in Canada and Jamaica for students and young people.

Work Canada

This scheme provides a general work permit valid for a six-month period which authorises the student to take up any job anywhere in Canada. To be eligible for this programme, applicants must be aged 18–29 and currently studying in full-time higher education in this country. Students in their gap year, and who are at least 18, can apply if they have an unconditional place in higher education for the following autumn. The fee for this programme is £79. In addition, it is necessary to pay for your own flight and insurance cover.

Work Jamaica

Work Jamaica enables participants to work anywhere in Jamaica for up to six months. It is open to those aged 19–35, who are full-time degree-level students. Gap-year students are not eligible. BUNAC provides a comprehensive list of employers who have hired BUNAC students previously and, on arrival in Jamaica, participants receive details of other employers who have expressed an interest in hiring Work Jamaica students. The price for the programme is £816 for June departures and £876 for July. This fee covers return flight, a work permit waiver granted by the Jamaican government, information sessions (orientation) in the UK and Jamaica, BUNAC administration costs, job listings, three months' insurance, first night's accommodation in Jamaica and support services in Jamaica. Completed application forms must be received by 29 March. It is advisable that interested applicants attend an information session before applying.

BUNAC also runs a Teach in Jamaica programme for graduates with accountancy, biology, chemistry, craft/design/technology, French, geography, maths, physics or Spanish degrees.

For more information about BUNAC work placements, contact BUNAC, 16 Bowling Green Lane, London EC1R 0BD (telephone: 0171-217 3472, fax: 0171-251 0215).

Emma Burnett

Work placements in Brazil and Japan case-study

Emma is 22 and, after her degree in architecture, she undertook two placements abroad. She spent three months in Brazil, via the IAESTE programme, and six months in Japan on a placement set up through her university. The work experience she undertook was part of the training required to go on to the postgraduate diploma in architecture.

‘I found out about IAESTE through a careers talk and sent my application in – three days before the deadline. Because I could speak Spanish, I applied for two placements in Spain but ended up going to Brazil which was better in the end as it was more adventurous.

In Brazil, I worked in a small architects' office drawing toilet, bathroom and window details, attending meetings and occasionally going out on site. The people in the office were very friendly and would always take time to explain things I didn't understand. I sometimes had problems expressing myself in Portuguese but I never felt lonely, or left out. It's amazing how much you can express with just a few words combined with careful pointing at things and mime.

IAESTE arranged a flat for me, which should have cost £20 a month, but the girl I was sharing with didn't want to take any money. I got the equivalent of 70p a day for working at the architects.

I really enjoyed my time in Brazil. I learnt a new language, made some strong friendships, and had my mind opened to a new way of life. I also saw the reality of poverty in the country and shared ideals and attitudes to life and architecture with the people I met.

After Brazil, I came back to the UK for three months and then set off again – this time to Japan. Again, I worked in a firm of architects and the placement was found for me by the head of my School of Architecture in the UK. All I had to do was send them a CV and a letter and I was accepted.

I went to Chinneru, a village of about 600 people, near Obihiro town on the island of Hokkaido. From the outset, myself and all the trainee architects in the office (four Japanese and me) were given similar responsibilities to the fully qualified architects.

For the first three months, I worked alone on a project producing preliminary schemes and presenting them to others in the office using drawings, diagrams and models. In the last three months, I was producing more detailed drawings for the clients and contractors; about 85 per cent of my time was spent designing and 15 per cent producing drawings. Looking back, I really feel I was given a lot of responsibility.

Some people were very friendly and others weren't. In the beginning, I really struggled with the language barrier and it affected my performance at work sometimes, especially when I wasn't told things. Fortunately, I got more used to Japanese and more people felt confident using English and, towards the end of my stay, it was good fun using pidgin language.

I was lonely and homesick at first – living and working in Japan was a big culture shock. It took a long time to make friends because of the language and cultural barriers and some people were pretty xenophobic. It did give me a stronger sense of independence though and, by the end, the Japanese and I felt much more comfortable with each other. I still keep in contact with the people in the office I worked in.

I really recommend degree-related placements abroad, even if they are only for three months. You learn about new cultures, pick up new languages, see different ways of working and get a chance to reassess long-term career plans. The placements I did gave me an excellent insight into the architectural profession and, through being able to see lots of different buildings around the world, I have developed a strong interest in practical construction issues.

In terms of professional training and advancement, the only disadvantage of gaining architectural work experience abroad is that you don't learn about the contractual, constructional and legal issues related to the English qualification which you learn if you do your work experience in the UK. I am now behind my colleagues who worked in the UK but I still have no doubts that my time abroad was worth it. ’

Council on International Educational Exchange (CIEE)

The Council on International Educational Exchange runs an Internship programme to the USA and Canada. Students on full-time sandwich courses in higher education, in which practical experience is an integral part, can spend up to a year on work experience in the USA and Canada. Students find their own placement which must be educational in nature and related to their course of study. CIEE will arrange all necessary documentation to obtain a visa from the US or Canadian embassies and provide orientation materials and support.

For more information, contact Council on International Educational Exchange, 33 Seymour Place, London W1H 6AT (telephone: 0171-706 3008).

Working in agriculture

If you want to work abroad, and you have a background in farming, the International Agricultural Exchange Association (IAEA) provides opportunities.

International Agricultural Exchange Association (IAEA)

Founded in 1963, the International Agricultural Exchange Association is a democratic, non-profit-making organisation that works closely with rural youth organisations and agricultural colleges in many of its member countries. These countries are Australia, Austria, Belgium, Canada, Denmark, Finland, France, Germany, Iceland, Japan, the Republic of Ireland, Latvia, Luxembourg, The Netherlands, New Zealand, Norway, Sweden, Switzerland, the United Kingdom and the USA. Participants have come from all these countries, although not all have reciprocal host families.

You can live with a host family in another part of the world and work with them in their agricultural or horticultural enterprises. It is a challenge that brings benefits educationally and personally. You have the chance to learn about agriculture in other parts of the world, try other ways of life and, if interested, learn a new language.

The programmes available vary in length from 6–14 months, although the longest stay in one country is nine months. From the UK, trainees travel to Australia, Canada, Japan, New Zealand and the USA.

Places are available in the categories listed overleaf.

Agriculture: Farm jobs are available; applicants must have good practical experience in general farming.
Agri-mix: You will work both on the farm and in the household, you must have some general practical experience and an interest in agriculture and home management.
Horticulture: You will work in orchards, greenhouses or with vegetables and need to have good practical experience in horticulture.
Horti-mix: You will work both with horticulture and in the household. You must have good general practical experience and an interest in home management.
Home management: You will work in the house and cook, clean, look after the children and help in the garden. You need to have good experience and an interest in general housekeeping.

Within each of these categories, you can choose the type of farm you would like to work on, eg dairy, sheep, beef, arable, fruit, vegetables or landscape gardening. IAEA aims to find you a host family which will best suit your experience, wishes and interests.

For each programme available, there is a total cost that covers all flights, airport taxes, insurances, stop-overs (these are usually in Bangkok, Singapore or Hawaii), transportation from point of arrival in host country to host family's farm, two-year membership of IAEA, pre-departure information meeting, orientation seminar in host country on arrival and IAEA administration fees.

While you are on the farm, you undertake paid work, being expected to do a five-day week, living as part of the family. All the programmes also include unpaid time off for holidays. This varies from 3–8 weeks according to the programme you choose.

For more information, contact IAEA UK Service Office, YFC Centre, National Agricultural Centre, Stoneleigh Park, Kenilworth, Warwickshire CV8 2LG (telephone: 01203 696578, fax: 01203 696684).

17 Work in the Community

There are many opportunities for voluntary work in the community overseas. Social and community projects available include working in deprived areas, working with children in an orphanage or with the disabled and teaching English as a foreign language. You could learn about community life by joining a workcamp or by living and working on a kibbutz in Israel.

Many of the organisations listed in this chapter concentrate on voluntary projects in the more deprived and poor areas of the world. All organisations expect applicants to be committed to the project they apply for. Most organisations recruit people who are 18 and above and experience is not usually required. People can volunteer for a few weeks or for more than a year; some organisations stipulate that volunteers stay a minimum length of time. Volunteers often have to pay for their own flight and in return they are provided with free board and accommodation and sometimes a small amount of pocket money. For some projects, volunteers have to pay the organisation a fee or raise sponsorship for the expedition. Sometimes, volunteers need to raise a few thousand pounds; the organisations will often give advice and help as to how this amount of money can be gathered. If you are interested in any of the volunteer opportunities in this chapter, you should start planning and applying early to give yourself enough time to raise the finance.

Some of the organisations listed here have already been mentioned in chapter 12 in Part 3. You may find it helpful to read chapter 18 also.

Africa Venture

Africa Venture provides hard-working school/college leavers who want to spend time in east Africa with constructive and rewarding work experience combined with companionship and adventure. Participants are placed in pairs as assistant teachers in selected Kenyan and Ugandan boarding schools for one or two terms. Depending on their skills and attributes, and the requirements of the school, they assist in a variety of subjects ranging from English, music and vocational activities to clubs and sports. Schools are chosen with location, work opportunities, accommodation and security in mind and placements do not deprive local Kenyan teachers from working. There are also opportunities for attachments to community-related projects such as orphanages or hospitals. Placements are usually for four months departing late August, early January or late April. Following the placement, participants have two weeks for independent travel and the complete programme is rounded off with a group safari to places of interest such as Lake Turkana or the Masai Mara Game Reserve.

Applicants should be a minimum of 17 and a half and should be studying A-levels, or the equivalent, and intending to go on to further study. They must be highly motivated, in good health and interested in working with young people of other cultures. Approximately 150 people are recruited each year.

The cost for applicants is approximately £1,550 which covers comprehensive health and personal effects insurance, orientation and in-country back-up, living allowance commensurate with local wages, self-catering accommodation in school grounds, all-inclusive safari and a contribution towards educating an African child. It does not cover the return air fare to Nairobi or extra spending money which are the responsibility of the participant. However, Africa Venture will organise the flight and offers very favourable fares (approximately £350). Africa Venture gives advice on raising sponsorship.

Interested applicants should apply early either by writing or telephoning. An information package and application form will be posted by return. Applicants will be invited to an interview where their suitability will be assessed. Those selected attend an orientation programme on arrival in Kenya or Uganda and have the support of the in-country Director throughout their stay.

For more information, contact the Director, Africa Venture, 10 Market Place, Devizes, Wiltshire SN10 1HT (telephone: 01380 729009, fax: 01380 720060).

ATD Fourth World

ATD Fourth World arranges long-term voluntary positions, for those over 18, to work with the needy in the Americas, Africa and Asia. Refer to the entry in chapter 12 for more details.

The Baptist Missionary Society (BMS)

The Action Teams offer opportunities for those aged 18–25 years to find out about life in a different country, share in practical work with a local Baptist church and be involved in their mission to the community around them.

From mid-September, teams of six get a month's training, then a full six months living in another part of the world followed by two months back in Britain sharing their experiences with churches and youth groups.

There are placements with church groups in Albania, Bangladesh, Brazil, El Salvador, India, Jamaica, Sri Lanka, Thailand and Zimbabwe. Participants contribute to travel and training expenses. BMS provides accommodation within Britain and the partner country.

For more information, contact the Missionary Support Manager, The Baptist Missionary Society, PO Box 49, Baptist House, 129 Broadway, Didcot, Oxfordshire OX11 8RT (telephone: 01235 512077).

Church Missionary Society (CMS)

CMS can help young Christians in the 18–30 age range to gain experience of a different culture through its Overseas Experience Camps. The summer camps are located in Africa, Asia and eastern Europe, and they provide an opportunity for young people to live alongside

Christians from another culture, sharing their lifestyle, witness, worship, hopes and aspirations.

Each group usually consists of ten participants with two experienced leaders who encourage the group to share and reflect together. The emphasis is put on the experience to be gained and not on the work contribution, although work projects are often part of the experience, eg tree planting, decorating a hospital, building a larder.

CMS also provides opportunities for people to gain experience of the church in a different culture through its Experience Placements Programme, either overseas or in the UK. This means that participants will be either working in the UK or alongside their partner churches in Asia, the Middle East, eastern Europe and in some African countries. The aim of the programme is not so much about giving as receiving and gaining cross-cultural experience while learning something about the church in another environment and having an opportunity to develop one's own personal faith in the light of these new experiences. By going on such a programme, young people may be better equipped to play a part in a world mission.

Participants need to be 21–30 at the start of an Overseas Experience Placement and between 18 and 30 at the start of a Britain Placement. The length of placements varies between 6 and 18 months. For visa purposes, a degree or professional qualification may be required to work in some countries, as well as having a real and living faith and the willingness to learn from other cultures and to share the experience with one's church and community on returning home.

CMS provides the cost of training but participants are responsible for other costs. The total cost of an overseas placement is approximately £1,500. For more information, contact the Experience Programme Adviser, Partnership House, CMS, 157 Waterloo Road, London SE1 8UU (telephone: 0171-928 8681).

GAP Activity Projects

GAP arranges voluntary opportunities, including social projects and TEFL placements, for gap-year students aged 18 and 19 in 33 countries worldwide. Countries include India and Indonesia. Refer to the entry in chapter 12 for more details.

Insight Nepal

According to Insight Nepal, 'Nepal is there to change you, not for you to change it. Lose yourself in its essence. Make your footprints with care and awareness of the precarious balance around you. Take souvenirs in your mind and spirit, not in your pockets. Nepal is not only a place on the map but an experience, a way of life from which we all can learn.'

Insight Nepal is an institution that was established with a view to introduce participants to Nepal's diverse geographical and cultural environment, and to establish and foster an awareness and understanding of cultural differences through experimental learning. Participants gain new skills, confidence and perspectives to create a new way of viewing the world by participating in Placement for Volunteer Service Work, which was started in 1994.

The institution provides an introduction or pre-orientation programme to Nepal which includes cultural tours, a family stay, Nepali language classes and country information for volunteers on arrival in Nepal before they join their project.

Applicants must be educated to at least A-level standard or equivalent, preferably with some teaching experience. Skills in games, sports or art are an advantage. The work involves teaching English, science, computer science, games and music in schools ranging from primary to technical schools. Half-board accommodation will be provided by the placement employer and one week's trekking is arranged. Volunteers can be placed in urban or remote areas of Nepal and placements can last one to four months. There are places for ten volunteers per placement date (four times a year). Completed application forms must be submitted at least two months in advance of the programme.

The costs to the applicant include a US$20 application fee (non-refundable), US$400 registration fee which covers pre-orientation/training and village excursion, visa fee, insurance and personal expenses and return air fare.

For more information, contact Naresh Man Shrestha, Director Insight Nepal, PO Box 6760, Kathmandu, Nepal (telephone: 00 977-1-418964, fax: 00 977-1-223515).

International Voluntary Service (IVS)

IVS organises workcamps in the former Soviet Union and the USA on social and environmental projects. For contact details, see the entry in chapter 8. Those interested in long-term volunteering in developing countries should contact Skillshare Africa, 3 Belvoir Street, Leicester LE1 6SL.

Involvement Volunteers Association Inc.

Involvement Volunteering is to travel and be involved in one or more volunteer activities related to the natural environment or social service in countries along the route. Individuals (or pairs, groups or teams) may apply to take part in activities in Europe and in Australia, California, the Central Americas, Fiji, Hawaii, India, Malaysia, New Guinea, New Zealand and Thailand. IVAI will be expanding into Africa in 1995/6. The benefits to the volunteer are that the experiences gained will assist them to test their choice for future education in short two-week placements or longer term 6–12 week placements, while at the same time gaining maturity and wisdom from international travel.

On payment of the initial application fee of AU$125 for 1994/5, potential volunteers receive a suggested programme of placements within their budget. The Involvement Volunteering newsletter is updated four times each year and sent to intending travelling volunteers to illustrate what is available for the coming year. To confirm acceptance of a programme with any number of

2–12 week Individual Volunteer Placements (IVPs) or Special Individual Volunteer Placements (SIVPs) the cost is AU$275. Pairs of volunteers participating and travelling together get a reduction. The placement fee for IVPs or SIVPs is AU$35 each. Group placements (GPs) and Team Tasks (TTs) cost from AU$75 per week. A cancellation fee of AU$35 for each placement is deducted from any placement fees to be refunded. Internal travel on mainland Australia (and islands off the coast) for IVAI's volunteers is available at a discount to take volunteers to placements, tourist areas and places of adventure along a travel route to combine touring with volunteering.

A PADI open-water scuba-diving course is available in Australia to IVI volunteers at a discount, providing four days with three nights on board a boat, out on the famous Barrier Reef. Sea-kayaking, white-water kayaking, surfing, snorkelling and sailing are some of the adventures available along the east coast that can be coupled with volunteering to create interesting holiday experiences in Australia.

Paid work is sometimes available in Australia or New Zealand to volunteers with suitable visas to meet local requirements and regulations. There will be places for 250 volunteers in 1995/6.

For further information, contact Involvement Volunteers Association Inc., PO Box 218, Port Melbourne, Victoria 3207, Australia (telephone/fax: 00 613 646 5504). IVI is also on the Internet. Its e.mail address is IVIMEL@IACCESS.COM.AU.

The Missions to Seamen

The Missions to Seamen organises voluntary work in the shipping industry for those 18 and above in Africa, Australia, the Far East, and the USA. Refer to the entry in chapter 13 for more details.

Operation Mobilisation

Operation Mobilisation is an international, interdenominational mission which has more than 2,500 people serving

God in evangelism, church planting (establishing a new church) and caring in co-operation with the local church in more than 60 countries. There are opportunities to swell these numbers by joining one of the Summer Challenge teams for between two weeks and two months. The emphasis of these teams is evangelism, creatively in mime, drama, sketchboard and children's clubs, in friendship through streetwork, hospital visits, youth work and coffee bars or through literature distribution on streets and door-to-door visiting. It is also possible to join a team for a year, broadening evangelism skills, helping to disciple new Christians and church plant in countries where the number of evangelical Christians is low. There are also opportunities for those with administrative skills to support the evangelism teams.

For more information, contact Operation Mobilisation, The Quinta, Weston Rhyn, Oswestry, Shropshire SY10 7LT (telephone: 01691 773388, fax: 01691 778378).

pro international e.V

This organisation arranges international workcamps for two to three weeks involving children's holidays, environmental and renovation work. Refer to the entry in chapter 13 for more details.

Project Trust

Volunteers work in social service projects such as orphanages, homes for physically or mentally disabled, at schools, on farms, with refugees and at outward bound schools. Projects are based in Africa, Australia, Central America, the Middle and Far East.

Applicants should be British, aged between 17 years and three months and 19 years and six months at the time of going abroad, and possess a high standard of intellectual and practical ability. They must be in full-time secondary/further education at the time of application.

The minimum length of service is one year and volunteers go abroad in August/September and return the following summer. Free board and accommodation are provided, and travel fares outside the UK and insurance are paid for by Project Trust. The cost per volunteer for 1995 is £3,450; £2,950 is raised by the volunteer, with help from Project Trust if necessary.

Approximately 200 volunteers are recruited annually. Applications should be made in writing and should be received by 1 November. Applicants attend preliminary discussions, which are held in various parts of the country, and are followed by a week's selection course on the Isle of Coll.

Simone Fox

Project Trust case-study

Before starting her psychology degree at Bristol University, Simone took a year out and went to Brazil with Project Trust.

‘I found out about Project Trust through another girl from school who had been to Honduras on their programme. I wanted to do something adventurous in my year out so I decided to apply. I had an interview in London and was then invited to a five-day selection course in Coll, an island off the coast of Scotland.

The selection course was enjoyable but tough and included language aptitude tests, essays, group and practical exercises. Project Trust tests your interaction with others and your strength of character; they need to be sure that you will be able to cope on a project overseas.

I got through the selection and luckily got my first choice of destination – Brazil. I then went on a four-day training course in Coll where I found out more about what I would be doing on the project. I met other students going to South America, including a girl who would be with me for the year. The training covered things like the politics and culture in Brazil, what to take, inoculations, potential difficulties and hazards.

My next step was to raise sponsorship for the project and I did this by arranging a mixed football match and writing to charities, the Rotary Club, the Lions Club, relatives and friends. It wasn't difficult raising the £2,500 I needed for the year (plus some money for travelling), and I got help from a variety of sources. When I was away, I sent a regular newsletter to all those who had helped me.

I flew out to Brazil in July with 17 other young people on Project Trust's programme. I was based in South Brazil in Rabeirao Preto, near São Paulo. My main project was teaching English in a school. This involved taking English conversation classes from 3pm to 7pm during the week. People attending the classes varied in ability and ranged from six years to 60. With the beginners, I played games and covered basic vocabulary but with the advanced groups I used newspapers and held discussions. I got paid the equivalent of about £60 a month.

I also arranged a secondary project in a crèche two mornings a week. I worked with children from very poor backgrounds who ranged from six months to 12 years. I helped with art classes, sports and games. I thoroughly enjoyed it.

In December, I had two months off and I travelled all around Brazil. I bought an air pass for £240, which entitled me to five flights anywhere in the country. There were some great beaches in the north-east. I also toured the Amazon for five days, saw some stunning waterfalls at Foz de Iguaçu, visited the swamplands in Pantanal and saw lots of wildlife. During one of my weekends, I also fitted in a trip to Rio.

I had a fantastic time travelling and met people from all over the world. Mind you, it can be risky and dangerous travelling around Brazil and my advice to others would be don't carry money or expensive items with you, be wary and sensible and don't take any risks.

I lived with two Brazilian families during my stay and food was provided. I didn't know any Portuguese but living with a family really helped me to pick it up. By the end of the year, I was pretty fluent in it. The families I lived with were very wealthy and our lifestyle contrasted starkly with that of many poor families in Brazil.

It was a brilliant year. I loved the country and enjoyed working, particularly in the crèche. I would recommend taking a year out with Project Trust. You gain confidence, experience the life and culture of another part of the world and do something exciting and worthwhile with your time. However, you do have your ups and downs and Christmas can be a difficult time. You must also plan well ahead to give yourself enough time to raise sponsorship and save money for your travels. ’

For more information, contact the Director, Project Trust, Hebridean Centre, Ballyhough, Isle of Coll, Argyll PA78 6TE (telephone: 018793 444).

Raleigh International

Raleigh International (formerly Operation Raleigh) is a charity that aims to develop young people by giving them the opportunity to carry out demanding environmental and community projects in the UK and around the world. Since 1984, 12,000 young people from 52 nations have taken part in 118 expeditions in 35 countries.

Raleigh International will recruit 1,000 young people, aged 17–25, from all walks of life, to undertake ten-week expeditions in Belize, Chile, Guyana, Uganda and Zimbabwe in 1995/6. Projects include diving on the Belize barrier reef, the construction of a clinic in Guyana and working on sight-restoration projects in Zimbabwe.

To qualify for a place on a Raleigh International expedition, all participants take part in a weekend of demanding problem-solving and team-working challenges. Participants are asked to raise a contribution towards the cost of the programme, which covers their air fares and in-country expenses. The amount varies according to personal circumstances. A series of fundraising events is being organised and some bursaries are available.

Lachlan Clark
Raleigh International case-study

Lachlan is now working as a field engineer with Schlumberger and spends a lot of time travelling abroad. In 1992, he graduated from university with a BEng in aeronautical engineering and decided to take a year out before starting employment.

❛I wanted to do something adventurous, challenging and exciting which would also involve contributing to the community, or preserving the environment. I also wanted to go abroad to experience a new environment and culture. I wanted a once-in-a-lifetime experience.

I heard about Raleigh International from friends and sent in an application. I was invited to a two-day selection course which involved building rafts and bridges, initiative exercises, cooking, giving a five-minute talk and taking part in a group discussion. It was very thorough but also great fun. The main quality needed was the ability to keep smiling regardless of the situation and despite not having had much sleep.

I got through the selection and ended up on a two-and-a-half month expedition to Guyana, in South America. Before going, I had to raise £2,950 through sponsorship and donations. The first half of the expedition was walking in the Kanuku mountains in the south of the country. We collected data on animals, insects, bird and plant life in an area which the locals rarely visited. Our group also spent two weeks building part of a school for a local village.

The second half of the trip was a medical project in the jungles in the north of the country. The villages we worked in could only be reached by canoe – there were simply no roads. We gave vaccinations to children and babies, did malaria smears and gave treatment, where necessary. We had two medics with our group. We spent a lot of our time just getting from place to place. A distance of 300 miles could take up to nine days – and could involve travel by lorry, boat, foot and LandRover. Travelling was no easy task; it was an adventure in itself!

The local villagers were shy at first but, once they were used to us, they were very friendly and generous with what little they had. We never wanted for fruit, or for somewhere to sleep. The Amerindians have a very different work ethic and perception of time to the UK; when they say something will happen "immediately", it could take two days!

Our team spent most nights sleeping in hammocks tied between trees. Everyone worked well as a team and most of the group were great though some were not what I would call best-friend material. I did make some very good friends, though, both from England and Guyana, and I am definitely going to keep in touch with them.

The trip was everything I had hoped for – adventure, excitement and challenge. I also learnt a lot about myself and feel that I have become a more patient and understanding person. You have to learn to be tolerant when you're living in close quarters with people for a long time. Of course, there were many problems and frustrations but that is partly what it was all about. Examples include a ferry arriving two days late, running out of fuel with the nearest fuel being two days' walk away, bricks arriving 14 days late and having to walk two miles to get more sand with only one-and-a-half wheelbarrows. The list goes on... but it was great fun.

By the end of the expedition, our group had a great sense of belonging; we had survived as a team for nearly three months despite some trying, uncomfortable and even potentially dangerous situations. I left the expedition feeling there is always someone in need of your help.

I would highly recommend Raleigh International. On the expedition I experienced the best three months of my life so far. You don't need any particular skills; you just need to be able to adapt to new situations and to keep smiling. You learn a great deal and return to the UK a changed person more aware of everything around you and seeking new challenges. It's the opportunity of a lifetime. ❜

Further information/application forms can be obtained from the Information Officer, Raleigh International, 27 Parson's Green Lane, London SW6 4HZ (telephone: 0171-371 8585).

The Right Hand Trust

The Right Hand Trust offers a gap-year experience living and working in Africa. Volunteers should be aged 18–30, be practising Christians and be available for eight months or longer. The trip includes a four-week holiday. Placements are available in Kenya, Uganda and Zimbabwe and activities range from teaching, paramedical and social work to administration and vocational training. Training for the work takes place in the UK before departure.

Volunteers need to raise money through sponsorship and employment to finance the trip which costs around £1,600 (this includes air fare, accommodation and insurance). Accommodation is simple and will probably be in a brick-built bungalow. There may not be electricity; water is probably from a standpipe and sanitation is communal. Furnishings are basic.

For more information, contact Right Hand Trust, Gelligason, Llanfair Caereinion, Powys SY21 9HE (telephone: 01938 810215).

St David's (Africa) Trust

St David's (Africa) Trust organises three- and six-month volunteer visits from January and September each year to help blind, orphaned and disabled children as well as animal healthcare work in Ghana, Morocco and Tunisia. Two to four students are required to work in a leper colony school on the Cape Coast 100 miles west of Accra in Ghana, up to 11 students are needed to work in a school for the disabled, a school for the blind and an orphanage in Taroudant at the foot of the Atlas

Mountains in southern Morocco and up to ten students are needed to work in a school for the deaf and dumb, a school for the blind and a kindergarten in Kelibia on the coast at Cap Bon in Tunisia.

Volunteers who work in Morocco or Tunisia spend half the day for six weeks learning Arabic and French and are then given further language training every three weeks at the weekend. English is spoken in Ghana so no language training is required.

Applicants must be a minimum of 18 years with an EU passport and (for north Africa) have a command of spoken French. St David's (Africa) Trust advises students on how to raise the money for the visit. There is a resident warden in the accommodation provided who looks after the volunteers. Projects starting in September last three months; those starting in January last six months.

For more information, contact David Denison, St David's House, Rectory Road, Crickhowell, Powys Wales, NP8 1DW (telephone and fax: 01873 810665 at any time).

United Society for the Propagation of the Gospel (USPG)
The USPG runs an experience exchange programme overseas which enables Christians to spend six months to a year experiencing the work of the church overseas in Africa, Asia or South America.

For more information, contact Short-term Experience Programme Officer, United Society for the Propagation of the Gospel, Partnership House, 157 Waterloo Road, London SE1 8XA (telephone: 0171-928 8681).

Volunteers with some experience

Below you will find details of two organisations that arrange voluntary placements for individuals with some relevant experience.

Voluntary Service Overseas (VSO)

VSO recruits volunteers who work in the fields of education, natural resources, the health services, technical trades and engineering, business and social work. Work takes place in over 50 developing countries in Africa, Asia, the Caribbean and the Pacific.

Applicants must be over 20 years (and under 70!) and have a degree, diploma or professional qualification. Additional work or experience is required in most cases. Applicants must be entitled to unrestricted entry to the UK and have no dependent children. The minimum length of service is two years. Approximately 750 qualified volunteers are taken on every year; just under 40 per cent of these work in education. Applications are accepted throughout the year.

VSO pays fares and various grants, health insurance and NI contributions. The overseas employer provides accommodation and a salary based on local rates.

Tony Beauchamp

Voluntary Service Overseas case-study

Tony had pursued a successful career teaching maths, and had reached the position of head of a middle school, when he decided that he wanted a change.

‘I took early retirement and was looking around for something interesting to do. I happened to see an advert for VSO in the *Times Educational Supplement* and decided to go along to an information evening for prospective volunteers. After that evening I was infected with enthusiasm. The room was full of interesting people, excited about life and about VSO.

I applied and attended an interview. This involved a series of character tests which test your organisational skills and assess how you relate to other people. I was prepared to go anywhere in the world and I was offered posts in Uganda and Bhutan.

I went to Uganda and taught maths to trainee teachers. It was really rewarding seeing my students going on to teach maths themselves, particularly knowing that when I first saw them most had great gaps in their knowledge.

I had a fantastic time; I met some really inspiring people

and I loved the climate. The Ugandans were generally optimistic about life because living standards were improving quickly and the country was gaining stability. I was initially going to stay for the minimum of two years but ended up staying for four. People were amazingly appreciative. Many people who volunteer for Uganda stay for more than the two years.

The college I worked for provided me with a three-bedroomed house. It had no running water and needed renovation but was just fine for me. I earned £80 a month – you can live on that fairly comfortably.

I made friends with many of the local people and learnt a smattering of the local language. There was also a good social life with the many other VSO volunteers in Uganda, and lots of opportunities to visit the capital Kampala.

Living in Uganda changed my whole way of looking at the developing world. I saw how people live and compared it to our standard of living. Many people can't afford to pay for simple drugs or treatments which would prevent them from dying from diseases that are easily curable.

One great feature of the posting was the long holidays, which meant I was able to travel all over Africa, and further afield. I visited Kenya, Tanzania, Zambia, Zimbabwe, Zaire, Zanzibar, Madagascar, Mauritius and India. I had some great times and fantastic experiences. One of the best was travelling down the River Congo in Zaire. The opportunity to travel is a big plus for VSO.

If people are considering VSO I would really recommended it. It is suitable for all ages. I met volunteers from the mid-20s to the 50s/60s. The experience enables you to gain a degree of self-confidence and learn how to look after yourself and relate to others. You also become more self-reliant, understanding and tolerant of others.

After four years, I came back to the UK and took an MA in computers in education. Now I'm looking forward to doing VSO again. I'm off to Pemba, off the coast of Tanzania, for two years more with VSO.
I can't wait. ’

Free VSO literature, giving details of skills and qualifications required and the terms of service, is available from the Enquiries Unit, VSO, 317 Putney Bridge Road, London SW15 2PN (telephone: 0181-780 2266).

Winant Clayton Volunteer Association

This is a summer programme from mid-June to mid-September, involving about eight weeks' work on the eastern side of the United States in urban situations. There are various programmes offering educational, recreational or therapeutic help ranging from children's play schemes, working with HIV/AIDS projects, psychiatric rehabilitation to work with the aged. Volunteers work alongside local people and are expected to be able to take considerable responsibility for planning and running their own programmes; they should have some experience of similar work in this country. About four weeks' free time is allowed for travel. Board, lodging and pocket money are provided. Small grants are paid towards the fare, but volunteers are asked to make a substantial contribution.

About 25 volunteers are recruited annually; applicants should be a minimum of 19 years old. Closing date for applications is mid-January. When writing, enclose a large SAE.

Steve Hill

Winant Clayton case-study

Steve left school after A-levels and went on to do an HND in Computing. After a short time, though, he realised that a career in computing was not for him, left college and returned home.

❝ I had always been interested in social work so I decided to look into voluntary opportunities with CSV. This led to me spending eight months working with young people in transitional accommodation in Kent. After this rewarding experience, I was inspired to look into voluntary work overseas and I decided to apply to Winant Clayton. I was successful at my interview and soon I was on my way to America with 20 other volunteers.

I was based in New York for two months. I worked for St Bartholomew's Church in a shelter for the homeless. The work was very varied and I loved it. Depending on the rota, I could be involved in setting out beds and staying at the shelter overnight; chatting to people; working on the breakfast feeding programme, which provided food for about 400 people in three hours; making sandwiches and serving food donated by local restaurants; working at the second-hand clothes closet; answering the phones; working in the stockroom or giving out prepacked food and tins at the pantry.

I had an apartment to myself, a luxury not afforded to all volunteers, and I was paid the equivalent of about £80 a week, which was adequate. I loved New York and had plenty of time off to visit the World Trade Centre, museums, places of interest and bars. I met up with the other Winant Clayton volunteers several times and we all spent a weekend at Long Island, paid for by the project.

I loved my new-found freedom and independence and would highly recommend the experience to others. However, volunteers have to be resourceful and sociable and not scared of being alone. Winant Clayton looks for a high level of commitment from volunteers.

After volunteering in New York, I spent five weeks travelling around America and visited Washington, New Orleans, Dallas, Virginia and San Francisco.

I am now back in the UK working full-time in a probation hostel. I feel that I was offered my present job as a result of my voluntary work in the UK and America. In the long-term, I would like to work with homeless people and, now that I've found a subject that inspires me, I may go back to college to take a social work qualification. ’

For more information, contact the Co-ordinator, Winant Clayton Volunteer Association, 38 Newark Street, London E1 2AA (telephone: 0171-375 0547).

Working on a kibbutz

A kibbutz is a rural communal settlement in Israel in which work, income and property are shared by its members. Kibbutz members (kibbutzniks) generally work within their community in agriculture, industry and the service areas, which include tourism, education, landscaping and kibbutz management. The work co-ordinator organises the daily work roster according to the needs of the kibbutz and each member's long-term work placement. Children are raised somewhat communally, in peer groups. They usually live with their parents, although some kibbutzim still have separate children's houses.

Kibbutzim in Israel have a reputation for hard work and, as a working visitor, you will be expected to work hard at whatever job is assigned to you, in return for the opportunity to participate in this unique lifestyle. Below, you will find the details of some organisations that can arrange for you to spend some time living and working on a kibbutz.

Friends of Israel Educational Trust

The Friends of Israel Educational Trust is a British charitable foundation formed to generate knowledge and interest in the land of Israel, its peoples and cultures. The charity was established in 1976 and is a non-denominational organisation.

The Bridge in Britain

The Bridge in Britain scholarship programme is sponsored by the Friends of Israel Educational Trust. The scheme is designed to promote a working knowledge, and a sympathetic understanding, of the problems and achievements of the State of Israel and its peoples. Up to 12 school/college-leavers are offered a passage to Israel and free board and lodging for five creative months in Israel. Those taking part must be over 18 and in good health; no knowledge of Hebrew is required.

Under the scheme, award winners are offered a working

place on a kibbutz, two months' community service in a development town, seminars and organised tours, as well as free time to travel around the country, and experience of an archaeological dig – now an optional extra at the participant's expense. The back-up of specialist helpers will be available throughout the period in Israel. Places are open to all, irrespective of sex, religion or creed.

All applicants have to explain their reasons for wishing to stay in Israel in a 400-word-minimum essay, to be submitted no later than 1 July each year. To apply, it is necessary to send a CV including date of birth, address, home telephone number, religion, academic achievements, interests and future plans, and a passport-size photo. Shortlisted candidates will be individually interviewed.

For more information, contact the Director, Friends of Israel, 25 Lyndale Avenue, London NW2 2QB (telephone: 0171-435 6803).

Kibbutz Representatives

Kibbutz Representatives runs a number of schemes including The Working Hebrew Scheme, which enables the participant to experience kibbutz life while providing the time to learn conversational Hebrew.

The Working Visitor Scheme

To apply, you need to be between 18 and 32 and be in good physical and mental health. You must be able to commit yourself for at least eight weeks. You will be expected to work hard, 6–8 hours a day, six days a week, at whatever is assigned to you, be it agricultural, industrial or in one of the services (ie dining room, laundry, clothes store, kitchen). You will be living two to four to a room, and the conditions could be fairly basic. You will be expected to conform to the regulations of the kibbutz while you are there. All applicants are interviewed.

In return for your commitment and hard work, you will receive food and lodging, laundry services, a small allowance and the recreational and other facilities that the kibbutz has to offer. There will also be the possibility of organised trips to places of interest. You will have the opportunity to experience an alternative lifestyle and your working holiday is likely to be an unforgettable experience.

It is essential to apply early as the scheme is popular. The application process can take between 3–5 weeks or longer in busy periods. Places for the summer are in high demand. Usually the minimum length of time you can spend on a kibbutz is eight weeks and the maximum is often three months. Any application to extend the stay needs to be made in Israel. The cost of this scheme is £45 registration, plus flight and insurance.

Anthony Silverstein

Kibbutz Representatives case-study

Anthony is currently studying for a degree in law, economics and European studies at the University of Hertfordshire. He took a year out after school to retake his A-levels and to have a break from study.

‘I contacted Kibbutz Representatives in April and, two-and-a-half weeks later, I was on a kibbutz in Rehovit, half an hour from Tel Aviv.

I expected the kibbutz to be basic and backwards, but was surprised to find that it was modern and clean with well-kept gardens and a pool. My accommodation, which I shared with two others was, however, very basic and not very clean but I soon got used to roughing it. Meals were provided in the kibbutz, and they were generally very good, and volunteers were given £32 a month to spend on the basic necessities.

I started off milking the cows with another volunteer. I thought that this was one of the worst jobs as you don’t meet many people. However, after I fractured my wrist while practising martial arts, I was moved to the apple factory and spent the rest of my time packing apples, plums and pears. I worked for six-and-a-half hours a day and for most of the time I was only able to use one hand.

I went out to the kibbutz with seven other volunteers and, in June, many more volunteers arrived from all over Europe, America, Canada and South Africa. I made some good friends and had a good social life. I also spent time talking to some of the kibbutzniks. Life on a kibbutz is peaceful and you have few worries. You do, however, have to pull your weight and work hard.

During my three months on the kibbutz, I managed to see a bit of Israel. I visited Jerusalem and Masada, the scene of a famous siege in Roman times, and swam in the Dead Sea.

I thoroughly enjoyed my time on the kibbutz and would recommend the experience. My advice to others planning to go would be don't take many clothes as it's hot, take plenty of toiletries and insect repellents as they are expensive, be prepared to pull your weight and be careful when travelling alone (females need to be especially careful). ’

For more information, contact Kibbutz Representatives, 1a Accommodation Road, London NW11 8ED (telephone: 0181-458 9235).

Project '67 Ltd

Project '67 arranges for volunteers to spend a minimum of eight weeks on a kibbutz in Israel. It also organises for individuals and groups to join archaeological digs on sites throughout Israel all year round. Experience is not essential but the qualities most needed are enthusiasm, the ability to mix and the willingness to accept a challenge. Applicants must be over 18 and fit. Prices from £214 include flights, insurance and board and accommodation. Project 67 also organises holidays in Egypt and Israel for the independent traveller and camel-riding trips in the Negev desert.

For more information, contact Project '67 Ltd, 10 Hatton Garden, London EC1N 8AH (telephone: 0171-831 7626).

18 Conservation and Renovation Work

There are many organisations through which you can take part in conservation and renovation work abroad. Some of these have already been mentioned in chapter 9 and you will probably find it useful to read chapter 13. The minimum age to take part varies between 16 and 18 and projects can last from a few weeks to a few months. You will usually need to pay for your travel and a fee may also be charged. Once abroad, accommodation and food may be provided.

Australian Trust for Conservation Volunteers (ATCV)
ATCV is the means by which voluntary manpower can be harnessed to benefit the environment. The Trust is concerned with environmental problems such as salinity, soil erosion, and loss of native habitat, native flora and fauna.

ATCV aims to promote practical conservation projects throughout Australia by involving people on a voluntary basis in the management and care of their environment, to assist local groups with management of conservation projects, to link landholders and volunteers in conservation-orientated projects, to develop training programmes for volunteers to acquire practical skills, to develop links with schools relating conservation projects to curriculum subjects and work experience, eg practical involvement on LandCare projects.

Overseas volunteers are invited to participate by undertaking an ECHIDNA Package. The ECHIDNA Package provides volunteers with the opportunity to undertake conservation projects with the ATCV. The minimum package is for six weeks, with the option to extend if vacancies are available.

ATCV has offices in Adelaide, Ballarat, Bendigo, Brisbane, Darwin, Melbourne, Sydney and Townsville. The ATCV was formed in Victoria in 1982 and has developed a well-organised and efficient infrastructure. In the last 12 months, ATCV volunteers have worked in Victoria, New South Wales, Tasmania, South Australia, Queensland and the Northern Territory.

For more information, contact Australian Trust for Conservation Volunteers, PO Box 423, Ballarat, Victoria 3353 (telephone: 00 61 53 331 483, fax: 00 61 53 332 290) and enclose two international coupons to cover return mail.

British Trust for Conservation Volunteers (BTCV)

BTCV organises conservation working holidays in the USA, Canada and Japan. Refer to chapter 9 for more details.

Coral Cay Conservation Ltd

Volunteer divers are required to join one of three international underwater survey projects to help establish management plans for the protection of threatened coral reefs in Turneffe Atoll (Caribbean), Danjugan Island (Philippines) and Dahlak Islands (Red Sea). One- to three-month expeditions are available throughout the year (prices from £1,725 fully inclusive). Dive training can be provided.

For more information, contact Coral Cay Conservation, 154 Clapham Park Road, London SW4 7DE (telephone: 0171-498 6248).

Earthwatch

Earthwatch organises over 850 science projects in 104 countries. Refer to chapter 9 for more details.

Frontier

Frontier is a non-profit-making organisation that brings together the conservation needs of developing countries with the commitment and enthusiasm of volunteers from around the world. At a time when ecological crises are multiplying and the resources to deal with them are diminishing, the Frontier initiative brings people aged 17 and over, untrained in conservation techniques, to the forefront of conservation research, enabling them to become involved in vital scientific work in the field.

Since Frontier's inception in 1989, well over 450,000 hours of research have been undertaken by volunteers in areas under threat in Tanzania, Uganda and Vietnam. Working alongside scientists and conservation organisations from these countries, each Frontier project represents a unique and valuable scientific investigation. Volunteers, who come from many backgrounds, spend ten weeks implementing a research programme that draws on their strengths as an expeditionary team. Unlike other organisations, the initiative comes from the volunteers themselves – a quality that is looked for when Frontier recruits volunteers.

If selected, volunteers are encouraged to participate in every part of the project, from data collection and surveys to fetching supplies from the local village. The 'hands-on' experience is such that many Frontier volunteers subsequently move on to work in conservation fields.

Each Frontier project is self-funded with the expeditionary team contributing to the cost of the expedition. Frontier volunteers are expected to raise between £2,600 and £2,900, which covers their air fare, insurance, accommodation and food in the field (which will be the local diet). Volunteers should also bring around £200 spending money to pay for drinks, meals out, postcards, stamps and souvenirs. Comprehensive advice on fundraising is made available to all potential volunteers. Frontier arranges a three-month visa/work permit which enables volunteers to spend 2–3 weeks travelling around the country they visit after the expedition.

For a free information pack and details of how to apply, contact Rachel Cornish, Frontier, 77 Leonard Street, London EC2A 4QS (telephone: 0171-613 2422).

United Nations Association (Wales) International Youth Service

This agency offers opportunities for volunteers to work

in hundreds of international volunteer projects in 30 countries on four continents. Each placement lasts 2–3 weeks and mostly involves manual conservation and renovation work though there are some social work projects. Volunteers, who must be 17 or over, must pay a fee and arrange their own transport to the project. Food, accommodation and insurance are provided. Most projects take place during July and August.

For more information, send an A5 SAE to United Nations Association (Wales) International Youth Service, Temple of Peace, Cathays Park, Cardiff CF1 3AP (telephone: 01222 223088).

19 Study Worldwide

Another option to consider is spending time abroad improving your language skills or studying a relevant course. Many graduate employers are now interested in applicants who have good language skills, or who have taken the initiative to study abroad. Studying abroad will bring you into contact with people of different nationalities and will broaden your horizons. A number of organisations offer opportunities to study abroad and Youth for Understanding, mentioned below, organises exchanges and paying guest visits abroad. Some of the organisations listed in this chapter are mentioned in more detail in chapter 14, which it is worth reading.

AFS Intercultural Education Programmes

AFS arranges for 15–18 year olds to spend a year in another country living as a member of a family and going to a local secondary school. Young people who take part in the programme usually go after GCSEs or A-levels, and after Highers or Sixth Year Studies in Scotland.

AFS students can go to one of 55 different countries, including Bolivia, Brazil, Chile, Columbia, Honduras, Indonesia, Panama, Paraguay, Thailand, the USA and Venezuela.

For more information, read AFS's entry in chapter 14 and contact AFS Intercultural Education Programmes, Ground Floor, Arden House, Wellington Street, Bingley, West Yorkshire BD16 2NB (telephone: 01274 560677, fax: 01274 567675).

Challenge Educational Services

Challenge Educational Services organises academic-year programmes for those aged 15–18 in schools in the USA. You will find more details on this organisation in chapter 14.

Council on International Educational Exchange (CIEE)

The Council on International Educational Exchange organises summer study courses in USA universities and also organises study abroad programmes from three to 56 weeks in various countries throughout the world. In addition to programmes in Europe (see chapter 14), study abroad programmes are run in Argentina, Australia, Brazil, Chile, China, Costa Rica, Dominican Republic, Ghana, Indonesia, Japan, Korea, Thailand and Vietnam. These programmes vary in level and are open to gap-year students, undergraduates, postgraduates and young professionals. Specific programmes for gap-year students are run in Australia, China, Costa Rica and Japan.

Programmes are of a very high quality and offer US university credit. Deadlines are at various points in the year, but applicants should contact CIEE no later than the start of their last year at school to have a full choice of courses. Fees apply to all programmes, but for students who are keen CIEE can offer assistance with fundraising activities.

For more details, contact Council on International Educational Exchange, 33 Seymour Place, London W1H 6AT (telephone: 0171-706 3008).

The English-Speaking Union of the Commonwealth

This organisation offers scholarships for school-leavers to spend two, or three, academic terms at American and Canadian independent schools. Scholarships are awarded in September for three terms and January for two terms. Students must have good general academic ability and show an interest in North American culture and society. Parents are asked to pay air fare and incidental expenses.

For more information, contact the Scholarships Manager, The English-Speaking Union, Dartmouth House, 37 Charles Street, London W1X 8AB (telephone: 0171-493 3328).

Experiment in International Living (EIL)

The Experiment in International Living, mentioned in more detail in chapter 14, can give information regarding a US University Placement Service for international students. This Placement Service assists students to apply for full-time or summer programmes. EIL is also the UK link for the International High School Programme in the USA which is open to 15–18 year old students. Students spend a year or a semester in the USA living with a family and attending school there.

For more details on the above programmes, contact Experiment in International Living, Otesaga, West Malvern Road, Malvern, Worcestershire WR14 4EN (telephone: 01684 562577).

Youth for Understanding (YFU)

YFU is a long-established international educational exchange organisation. Exchange students from the UK can go to the USA for a year, live with a host family and attend school there. Alternatively, they can choose to go to Japan for six months. In the near future, UK students will also be able to go to Australia and New Zealand for six months. Students who choose Japan will spend time learning the language and many will come back able to speak fluently.

The exchange programme is open to young people aged between 16 and 18. The cost of the programme to the USA is £3,750 and to Japan is £4,000. The New Zealand programme will start in January 1996 and exchanges will be for six months. The cost for participants will be £3,200. The Australia programme will start in January 1997 and exchanges will be for six months. The cost for participants will be no more that £3,500. Early application is advisable.

For further details, please read the YFU entry in chapter 14.

Learn to ski

For something a little less academic, you might consider learning to ski in Canada.

Ski Le Gap – Laurentian Ski School

Ski Le Gap runs courses which enable gap-year students to qualify as ski instructors and improve their French. The ski school is situated amidst the Laurentian Mountains in the French-speaking town of Ste Agathe des Monts in Quebec. Students are accommodated in comfortable, traditional Canadian-style houses and breakfast and evening meals are provided.

Courses last either one or three months. Intensive daily instruction is given by ski instructors from the Canadian Ski Instructors Alliance (CSIA). The emphasis is on working towards a CSIA qualification. The examination for the CSIA involves a multi-day assessment by the Independent National Ski Association. Students are not guaranteed a pass and they will be advised which level of certificate they should be entered for.

Depending on their prior ski experience, students who complete the one-month course can reach up to level one. Those on the three-month course can achieve levels one or two. Level one enables people to work as ski instructors. Past students, who have achieved a good level, have gone on to work in New Zealand, Japan, Canada and America. However, competition for ski instructor positions is fierce.

The courses also encourage students to speak and to improve their French. Language courses are offered.

The cost of the one-month course is £1,500 and the three-month course is £3,500 (1994/5). This price includes return air fare London–Montreal, half-board and lodging (breakfast and evening meals), ski passes, instruction in Alpine and Nordic ski courses (the one-month course offers only Alpine ski instruction), and French conversation course.

Anita Graham and Charlotte Stretton were students at the Laurentian Ski School in 1994.

Anita Graham

'Spending three months in the mountains of Quebec seemed like a dream – but it was hard work. The ski instruction is given by highly qualified instructors who certainly know how to push you; the course is not for the lazy skier.

I gained my level one CSIA at the end of three months and then taught skiing in both Canada and the USA. Another student spent four months teaching skiing in New Zealand and another was offered a job in Japan.

It is hard to put down all the special times we had, or to explain the memories. We worked hard together and we had fun together. Three months is long enough to form very strong friendships, especially when you are all working together at something that everyone enjoys.'

Charlotte Stretton

'The snow was the deepest I'd ever seen, the instruction the most relevant and professional I've ever experienced, the accommodation as warm as a sauna. After a day's skiing, we would come back, sit in front of a blazing log fire, eat toasted muffins and analyse the video of our skiing. The emphasis on personalised tuition from the level four CSIA instructor was undoubtedly the key factor in the 100 per cent pass rate of all who took the level one exam.'

For more information, contact Fiona Little, Laurentian Ski School, c/o Giacometti, 43 Bedford Street, London WC2E 9HA (telephone: 0171-379 6551).

20 Travel, Exploration and Adventure Worldwide

You may have a taste for travelling to far-flung regions of the world and, if this is the case, there are a number of travel options you can consider.

Expeditions

If you can raise the finances and sponsorship, you could spend a few months on an expedition in one of the developing regions of the world. This would involve group travel and you could be involved in a social or environmental project. Raleigh International, mentioned in chapter 17, is a well-known organisation that arranges expeditions for young people. Information on other expeditions can be found in *The Traveller's Handbook* published by WEXAS International, mentioned below.

Organised adventurous and exploratory travel

There are a number of tour operators that specialise in organising small group exploratory holidays and adventurous travel to areas in Asia, Africa and South America. Some well-known names include Explore (telephone: 01252 344161), Exodus (telephone: 0181-673 0859) and Encounter Overland (telephone: 0171-373 1433). Other well-established operators are Dragoman, Guerba and Trek America for which Trailfinders, an independent travellers' agency in London (telephone: 0171-938 3366), is agent. There are also many other smaller operators which are worth checking out. You will usually find them advertising in the Sunday newspapers.

Independent travel

You may decide to go it alone and to organise your travels independently. If this is what you decide, make sure that you plan ahead and that you have enough money to finance your travels. Trailfinders deals with long- and short-haul around-the-world itineries. There are many other travel agents, usually based in London, that specialise in cheap long-haul flights. Some such as STA Travel, Campus Travel, and the Council on International Educational Exchange (mentioned in more detail in chapter 15) particularly specialise in student travel. When booking a flight you need to shop around.

Planning your trip

There will be many things you need to think about and arrange if you will be travelling to less developed regions of the world. Some of the main areas you need to think about are covered below.

Insurance

Before travelling, it is important to arrange a comprehensive travel insurance covering medical treatment and loss of personal belongings. ISIS (International Student Insurance Service) provides reasonably priced insurance cover for young people. Details of ISIS are available from Endsleigh Insurance Services Ltd, Endsleigh House, Ambrose Street, Cheltenham, Gloucestershire GL50 3NR. Columbus Insurance Services Ltd in London (telephone: 0171-225 1733) specialises in travel insurance. Shop around for the best coverage and price.

Accommodation

Read chapter 15 for information on the Youth Hostels Association and Young Men's Christian Association. There are also a number of good guide books mentioned in chapter 15 which are specially written for budget travellers and they have detailed infor-mation on places to stay and prices.

ISIC card

Please read chapter 15 for information on the ISIC card.

Visas

You will usually need to organise visas to enter most countries outside Europe. In some cases, you will need to arrange the visa before you enter the country, either in the UK or in the country you visit previously. Sometimes, you will be issued with a visa on entry to the country and will be allowed to stay there for a few months. In many countries, visas issued will just allow you to travel. Work visas will normally be more difficult to arrange. Before you go, check visa requirements with the relevant embassies based in London (see Country Index in Part 5).

Inoculations

For many countries, particularly in Asia, South America and Africa, you will need to have inoculations such as tetanus, hepatitis and polio and you will need to take malaria tablets with you. Often you will need a month or longer to have the inoculations so make sure you think about this early. Check inoculations required with your GP or ring the MASTA (Medical Advisory Services for Travellers Abroad) travellers' helpline. MASTA is a database validated by the London School of Hygiene and Tropical Medicine. The number to call is 0891 224100 and lines are open 24 hours a day. You will be sent a health brief specifically tailored to your journey and will be given information about immunisations, as well as any Foreign Office advice and latest health news.

Finance

You will need to ensure that you have enough money with you to pay for travel and accommodation and a bit extra just in case you are ill or have an accident. This will usually mean that you will have to work before you go or pick up jobs while you are travelling. It is safer to take traveller's cheques with you if you will be travelling in areas where there is a high crime rate and where pick-pocketing is rife. If you keep details of all your traveller's cheques they can be replaced if they are stolen. A

Visa or Access card can be useful if you get into financial difficulties. To avoid this, though, try to calculate how much you're likely to spend by finding out approximate costs of travel and accommodation and by researching the costs of living in the countries you intend to travel to.

Safety

Read up about the countries you will be visiting before setting off and be careful. In some of the recommended travel guide books you will find particular sections on hazards for women travellers. Make sure that you are aware of things to watch out for and don't trust people who are overly friendly.

Useful things to take with you

Below is a list of some of the things you might need to take, particularly if you are going to tropical countries:

- rucksack
- money belt
- sheet sleeping bag
- padlock
- malaria tablets
- medical kit including sterile needles
- rehydration mixture (for severe diarrhoea)
- vitamin tablets
- flip-flops
- traveller's cheques
- Visa/Access card
- Swiss Army penknife
- mosquito repellent (in some countries a mosquito net or mosquito plug to use in your room at night could be useful)
- sunscreen and aftersun lotion
- guide books
- water purifying tablets
- salt tablets
- sunhat
- walking shoes.

Useful sources of information

WEXAS International

Worldwide travellers might be interested in joining Wexas International Ltd. This organisation makes awards totalling £2,000 to approved group expeditions through the Royal Geographical Society Award Scheme.

Members of WEXAS benefit from special rates for immunisation, flights, insurance, hotels and car hire, as well as having access to Discoverers' holidays and receiving *Traveller* magazine. The World Discoverers' Programme combines a unique selection of round-the-world customised flights and tours with a wide-ranging collection of trips that go beyond the run of the mill. Information on these holidays is available in the brochure *World Discoverers.* WEXAS also publishes *The Traveller's Handbook* (available at discount to members).

The Traveller's Handbook provides information on expeditions and adventure holidays plus advice for the independent traveller. Its 940 pages include details on how to plan a trip, where to go, airline tickets, what equipment you will need, where to stay, what to do when things go wrong, eg theft, hijacking, jungle survival. There are also 10,000 helpful names and addresses including consulates and organisations that arrange expeditions and adventure holidays. The book currently costs £14.95 and is available from bookshops.

WEXAS International is based at 45–49 Brompton Road, Knightsbridge, London SW3 1DE (telephone: 0171-589 0500/3315).

5

Appendices

Reading List

This reading list has been grouped by theme for ease of reference.

Options

A Year Between, Central Bureau for Educational Visits and Exchanges, Seymour Mews, London W1H 9PE (telephone: 0171-486 5101), £8.99.

Opportunities in the Gap Year, ISCO, 12a Princess Way, Camberley, Surrey GU15 3SP (telephone: 01276 21188), £3.50.

Scholarships and sponsorship

Charities Digest, published by Family Welfare Association, 501–505 Kingsland Road, Dalston, London E8 4AU (telephone: 0171-254 6251). Provides details and addresses of some 1,200 national and regional charities in the UK including details of organisations related to health and social welfare, housing, education and the environment as well as grant-making trusts and sources of help for people in need. Also details on councils for voluntary service and volunteer bureaux.

Directory of Grant-Making Trusts, published by Charities Aid Foundation, 48 Penbury Road, Tunbridge, Kent TN9 2JD (telephone: 01732 771333). Most of the entries are relevant to charities applying to other charities for financial aid. There are, however, a small number of charities that may help with educational grants.

Engineering Sponsorships is free and can be requested from the Engineering Council, 10 Maltravers Street, London WC2R 3ER (telephone: 0171-240 7891). Send an SAE with an 80p stamp.

Everything You Wanted to Know About Sponsorship, published by Amoeba Publications, Lakeside Manor Farm, Crowland Road, Eye Green, Cambridgeshire PE6 7TT (telephone: 01733 223113). Contains 100 A4 pages of advice about getting sponsorship and scholarships plus advertisements totalling £2.5 million worth of sponsorship. Sponsorships for most degree courses (except music and dance); the majority of sponsorships are for science and engineering courses.

Money to Study, Family Welfare Association, 501–505 Kingsland Road, Dalston, London E8 4AU (telephone: 0171-254 6251). Currently out of print but may be updated; covers grants, loans, welfare benefits, sponsorship, scholarships, trusts and charitable help, money management and debt.

Postgraduate Awards, available free from the Department for Education Publications Centre, PO Box 2193, London E15 2EU (telephone: 0181-533 2000).

Sponsorship and Donations Yearbook, published by Hollis Directories Ltd, Contact House, Lower Hampton Road, Sunbury-on-Thames, Middlesex TW16 5HG (telephone: 01932 784781). The definitive guide to the UK's top sponsoring and donating companies, sponsorship opportunities, specialist consultancies and services.

Sponsorship for Students, available from COIC, PO Box 348, Bristol BS99 7FE (telephone: 0117-977 7199) for all students seeking sponsorship for degree/HND courses, £5.

Sports Scholarships and College Athletic Programs in the USA, Vacation Work, 9 Park End Street, Oxford OX1 1HJ (telephone: 01865 241978), £17.95.

Students' Money Matters, published by Trotman & Company, 12 Hill Rise, Richmond, Surrey TW10 6UA (telephone: 0181-332 2132), £6.95. Information on finance for students including sponsorships and bursaries.

The Grants Register, published by Macmillan Press Ltd, Houndmills, Basingstoke, Hampshire RG21 2XS (telephone: 01256 29242). This is primarily targeted at undergraduates/graduates who require further professional or advanced vocational training. The register includes a wealth of information including details on scholarships, fellowships and research grants, exchange opportunities, vacation study awards and travel grants, grants-in-aid, grants for artistic or scientific projects, competitions, prizes and honoraria, professional and vocational awards and special awards (for refugees, minority groups, etc) and funds for students in unexpected financial difficulties.

Paid employment

The Au Pair and Nanny's Guide to Working Abroad, £8.95 paperback, £14.95 hardback.
Directory of Summer Jobs Abroad, £7.95 paperback, £12.95 hardback.
Directory of Summer Jobs in Britain, £7.95 paperback, £12.95 hardback.
Emplois D'Eté en France, £7.95.
All published by Vacation Work, 9 Park End Street, Oxford OX1 1HJ (telephone: 01865 241978).

Getting a Job in Europe, Northcote House Publishers Ltd, Plymbridge House, Estover Road, Plymouth, Devon PL6 7PZ (telephone: 01752 695745), £7.99.

How To Become an Au Pair
How To Find Temporary Work Abroad
How To Get a Job in Europe
*How To Live and Work in America**
How To Live and Work in France
How To Study Abroad
How To Teach Abroad
How To Teach English as a Foreign Language
All £8.99 (except * £9.99) and all available from How To Books Ltd, Plymbridge House, Estover Road, Plymouth, Devon PL6 7PZ (telephone: 01752 695745).

How To Get a Job in Europe also available from Hobsons Publishing PLC, Bateman Street, Cambridge CB2 1LZ (telephone: 01223 354551).

Internships USA, Vacation Work, 9 Park End Street, Oxford OX1 1HJ (telephone: 01865 241978), £19.95.

Live and Work in... France, Spain & Portugal, Italy, Germany, Benelux, Scandinavia, USA & Canada, Australia & New Zealand, Vacation Work, 9 Park End Street, Oxford OX1 1HJ (telephone: 01865 241978), £7.95–8.95 paperback, £10.95–14.95 hardback.

Summer Jobs USA, Vacation Work, 9 Park End Street, Oxford OX1 1HJ (telephone: 01865 241978), £10.95.

Teach Abroad, Central Bureau for Educational Visits and Exchanges, Seymour Mews, London W1H 9PE (telephone: 0171-486 5101), £8.99.

Teaching English Abroad, Vacation Work, 9 Park End Street, Oxford OX1 1HJ (telephone: 01865 241978), £9.95 paperback, £15.95 hardback.

Work Experience Abroad, published by the British Council and available from the British Council Information Centre, 10 Spring Gardens, London SW1A 2BN (telephone: 0171-389 4383).

Working in Tourism: The UK, Europe and Beyond, Vacation Work, 9 Park End Street, Oxford OX1 1HJ (telephone: 01865 241978), £15.95 hardback.

Work Your Way Around the World, Vacation Work, 9 Park End Street, Oxford OX1 1HJ (telephone: 01865 241978), £9.95 paperback, £15.95 hardback.

Working Holidays, Central Bureau for Educational Visits and Exchanges, Seymour Mews, London W1H 9PE (telephone: 0171-486 5101), £8.99.

Working in... (all EU countries), published by the Overseas Placing Unit, 4th Floor, Skills House, 3–7 Holy Green, The Moor, Sheffield S1 4AQ (telephone: 0114 259 6051/2).

Working in Ski Resorts. Europe & North America, Vacation Work, 9 Park End Street, Oxford OX1 1HJ (telephone: 01865 241978), £8.95 paperback, £14.95 hardback.

Voluntary work

How to Do Voluntary Work Abroad, How To Books Ltd, Plymbridge House, Estover Road, Plymouth, Devon PL6 7PZ (telephone: 01752 695745), £8.99.

Kibbutz Volunteer, Vacation Work, 9 Park End Street, Oxford OX1 1HJ (telephone: 01865 241978), £5.95 paperback, £8.95 hardback.

The International Directory of Voluntary Work published by Vacation Work, 9 Park End Street, Oxford OX1 1HJ (telephone: 01865 241978), £8.95 paperback.

Voluntary Agencies Directory, available from the National Council for Voluntary Organisations, Regent's Wharf, 8 All Saints Street, London N1 9RL (telephone: 0171-713 6161), £15.95 plus £1.60 packing and postage. Your local reference library should hold a copy.

Volunteer Work, Central Bureau for Educational Visits and Exchanges, Seymour Mews, London W1H 9PE (telephone: 0171-486 5101), £8.99.

Study

Erasmus: the UK guide 1995, ISCO, 12a Princess Way, Camberley, Surrey GU15 3SP (telephone: 01276 21188), £9.40 plus £1.10 p & p.

Higher Education in the European Community: the student handbook (Commission of the European Communities), published by Kogan Page and available from HMSO Bookshop, 49 High Holborn, London WC1V 6HB (telephone: 0171-873 0011), £14.95.

Home from Home, Central Bureau for Educational Visits and Exchanges, Seymour Mews, London W1H 9PE (telephone: 0171-486 5101), £8.99.

Study Abroad, published by UNESCO and available from HMSO Bookshop, 49 High Holborn, London WC1V 6HB (telephone: 0171-873 0011), £13.25.

Study Holidays, Central Bureau for Educational Visits and Exchanges, Seymour Mews, London W1H 9PE (telephone: 0171-486 5101), £8.99.

Studying Abroad, published by the British Council and available from the British Council Information Centre, 10 Spring Gardens, London SW1A 2BN (telephone: 0171-389 4383). The British Council can provide some information on scholarships abroad. These are primarily postgraduate scholarships.

Studying in Europe, available from Hobsons Publishing PLC, Bateman Street, Cambridge CB2 1LZ (telephone: 01223 354551), £8.99.

The European Choice: a guide to opportunities for higher education in Europe, published by the Department for Education. Provides some useful information and can be ordered from the Department for Education Publications Centre, PO Box 2193, London E15 2EU (telephone: 0181-533 2000).

Travel

Adventure Holidays, Vacation Work, 9 Park End Street, Oxford OX1 1HJ (telephone: 01865 241978), £5.95 paperback, £10.95 hardback.

How to Travel Round the World, How To Books Ltd, Plymbridge House, Estover Road, Plymouth, Devon PL6 7PZ (telephone: 01752 695745), £8.99.

The Traveller's Handbook, published by WEXAS International, 45–49 Brompton Road, Knightsbridge, London SW3 1DE (telephone: 0171-589 0500/3315), £14.95.

Country Index

Useful information on working, studying and travelling in Europe and worldwide can be gathered by contacting embassies, cultural institutes and some tourist offices. When contacting embassies, you will need, in most cases, to ask to speak to the labour office for information on employment and the cultural or education department for information on study. Generally, embassies can provide information relating to employment in the country they represent but most do not deal with job vacancies. They usually provide information on study and language courses.

COMMONWEALTH COUNTRIES

The Association of Commonwealth Universities
John Foster House
36 Gordon Square
London WC1H 0PF
Telephone: 0171-387 8572
The Association provides details of universities, entry, application, fees, awards, scholarships, fellowships and bursaries for those wanting to study at university in a Commonwealth country in Africa, Asia, Australasia and the South Pacific, in Canada and the Caribbean, Cyprus and Malta.

AUSTRALIA

Australian High Commission
Australia House
Strand
London WC2B 4LA
Telephone: 0171-379 4334
The High Commission provides general information for people wanting to enter Australia. It keeps newspapers and telephone books for those wanting to apply to

companies in Australia. Those requiring visa information can call in to the visa department for information. For information on matters relating to work, study and visas, telephone 0891 600333. For information on temporary entry – temporary resident, student and visitor visas – telephone 0171-887 5320/5637.

Australian Outlook
3 Buckhurst Road
Bexhill on Sea
East Sussex PN40 1QF
Contact Australian Outlook to order a working holiday application form.

AUSTRIA

Anglo-Austrian Society
46 Queen Anne's Gate
London SW1H 9AU
Telephone: 0171-222 0366
Besides specialising in travel to Austria, the Society can book budget flights to selected European destinations including Munich, Zürich, Budapest and Prague. The society also offers German language courses, school holiday exchanges and youth group travel.

Austrian Embassy
18 Belgrave Mews West
London SW1X 8HU
Telephone: 0171-235 3731
The embassy provides information on employment in Austria. Its leaflet explains employment opportunities, the necessity of a sound knowledge of German, social security, tax, work and resident permits. In 1995, Austria joined the European Union so work permits are not required for EU nationals. The embassy provides a list of employment offices in Austria and refers people to the Austrian Committee for International Educational Exchange (ÖKISTA), Garnisongasse 7, 1090 Vienna, Austria for information on short-term or holiday employment in Austria.

Austrian Institute
28 Rutland Gate
London SW7 1PQ
Telephone: 0171-584 8653
The Institute provides information on the culture, economics and geography of Austria as well as information on studying in higher education in Austria and language courses. It also provides limited information on employment and will send out a list of employment agencies. It has a library that is open to the public.

Austrian National Tourist Office
30 Saint George Street
London W1R 0AL
Telephone: 0171-629 0461

Österreichische Hochschülerschaft
(Austrian National Union of Students)
Liechtensteinstrasse 13
1090 Vienna
Austria
Telephone: 00 43 1 310 8880
The Union can advise students on studying in Austria.

Österreichische Komitee für Internationalen Studienaustausch (ÖKISTA)
(Austrian Committee for International Educational Exchange)
Garnisongasse 7
1090 Vienna
Austria
Telephone: 00 431 401 48 225 or 226
ÖKISTA organises international educational exchanges.

BELGIUM

Belgian Embassy
103 Eaton Square
London SW1W 9AB
Telephone: 0171-235 5422

The embassy can provide information on language and other courses in Belgium, equivalence of diplomas and scholarships for postgraduate research.

Belgian Tourist Office
5th Floor
29 Princes Street
London W1R 7RG
Telephone: 0171-629 0230

CANADA

Canadian High Commission
Macdonald House
1 Grosvenor Square
London W1X 0XB
Telephone: 0171-258 6600
The High Commission provides information on immigration procedures and general information on universities in Canada and awards for British graduate students.

Canadian Bureau for International Education
220 Laurier W/O
Suite 1100
Ottawa
Ontario K1P 5Z9
Canada
Telephone: 00 1 613 237 4820
The Bureau provides two information leaflets, *Study in Canada* and *Awards for Study in Canada*, for foreign students (no charge and written in English, French and Spanish). It also produces a guidebook in English and French called *International Students' Handbook* which costs CAN$10 post-paid.

CZECH REPUBLIC

Czech Republic Tourist Office
30 Kensington Palace Gardens
London W8 4QY
Telephone: 0171-243 7981

DENMARK

Danish Tourist Board
55 Sloane Street
London SW1X 9SY
Telephone: 0891 600109

Royal Danish Embassy
Information Office
55 Sloane Street
London SW1X 9SR
Telephone: 0171-333 0200/235 1255
The embassy provides information on living, working, studying and learning Danish in Denmark.

FINLAND

Finnish Embassy
38 Chesham Place
London SW1X 8HW
Telephone: 0171-838 6200
The embassy provides information on short-term study and work exchanges in Finland. It can also advise on language courses.

Finnish Institute
35–36 Eagle Street
London WC1R 4AJ
Telephone: 0171-404 3309
The Institute provides information on international programmes (taught in English), student and staff exchanges and research grants and scholarships. It can also give out information on where people can study Finnish and what kind of courses are available.

FRANCE

Accueil des Jeunes en France
This organisation helps young people find accommodation, including youth hostels, and can arrange flights, bus and train travel for young people. There are five youth hostels in Paris and many throughout France as a whole. Accueil des Jeunes en France can be contacted opposite.

For groups only (ten persons and above):
16 rue du Pont Louis Philippe
F75004 Paris
France
Telephone: 00 33 1 42 72 72 09

For individuals:
119 rue St Martin
F75004 Paris
France
Telephone: 00 33 1 42 77 87 80

139 boulevard St Michel
F75005 Paris
France
Telephone: 00 33 1 43 54 95 86

From July to September:
Gare du Nord
Paris
France
Telephone: 00 33 1 42 85 86 19

ANPE (Agence National Pour Emploi)
Le Galilée
93198 Noisy le Grand
Paris
France
Telephone: 00 33 1 46 27 79 74
ANPE is the national Employment Service and there are branches in most main towns and cities. It will give you advice and provide you with job vacancies or work placements. You will not need a work permit to work in France but will need to apply for a resident's permit. Residence permit application forms are available in police stations.

Le Centre d'Information et de Documentation de la Jeunesse (CIDJ)
101 Quai Branly
75740 Paris cedex 15
France
Telephone: 00 33 1 44 49 12 00
The CIDJ has a file of information for foreigners coming to Paris which includes details on short-term and long-term work, au pair work, study, summer courses, language courses and other organisations which can help foreigners in Paris. CIDJ produces a whole range of publications covering entry and training for a multitude of careers. In particular, it publishes a leaflet *Recherche d'une job* for young people looking for summer employment.

La Cité des Métiers et de l'Industrie
30 avenue Corentin-Cariou
75930 Paris
France
Telephone: 00 33 1 40 05 85 85
Provides careers information and has representatives from ANPE on site.

French Embassy
Cultural Department
23 Cromwell Road
London SW7 2EL
Telephone: 0171-838 2055
The embassy can provide information regarding learning French and working holidays in France (for information please write with an SAE).

French Government Tourist Office
178 Piccadilly
London W1V 0AL
Telephone: 0891 244123

Manpower
9 rue Jacques Bingen
75017 Paris
France
The employment agency Manpower has over 600 branches around Paris and throughout France. However, for most of their vacancies a good knowledge of French and a year's relevant work experience are required. To apply for their vacancies you must already be living in France.

GERMANY

The Anglo-German Association
158 Buckingham Palace Road
London SW1W 9TR
Telephone: 0171-259 9922
This charity encourages Anglo-German friendship and understanding through education, culture and social events.

Artu Berliner Gesellschaft für Studenten und Jugendreisen GmbH
Hardenbergstraße 9
10623 Berlin
Germany
Telephone: 00 49 30 310 00 40
This travel agency caters specially for young people in Germany.

German Academic Exchange Service
17 Bloomsbury Square
London WC1A 2LP
Telephone: 0171-404 4065
The Exchange Service supplies a list of language courses and university vacation courses in Germany. It also provides information on scholarships for study and research in Germany.

The German–British Chamber of Industry and Commerce
Mecklenburg House
16 Buckingham Gate
London SW1E 6LB
Telephone: 0171-233 5656
The Chamber of Industry and Commerce can provide information for businesses. When requesting information, enclose a large SAE.

German Embassy
Cultural Department
23 Belgrave Square
London SW1X 8PZ
Telephone: 0171-235 5033
The embassy provides general background information on Germany relating to its politics, culture, society and economics. No information is provided on finding employment.

German National Tourist Office
Nightingale House
65 Curzon Street
London W1Y 8NE
Telephone: 0891 600100

GREECE

Embassy of Greece
1a Holland Park
London W11 3TP
Telephone: 0171-221 6764
The Greek embassy education department (0171-221 0093) can provide information on the educational system in Greece and language courses. The cultural department (0171-229 3850) can provide information on higher education in Greece, lists of universities, information on scholarships and details on institutions teaching Greek to foreigners in Greece. The labour department (telephone: 0171-221 6764) provides information on working in

Greece and gives addresses and telephone numbers of Greek organisations. For information, send an SAE.

National Tourist Organisation of Greece
4 Conduit Street
London W1R 0DJ
Telephone: 0171-734 5997

HUNGARY

Embassy of the Republic of Hungary
46 Eaton Place
London SW1X 8AL
Telephone: 0171-235 8767/9
Contact the embassy for information regarding work permits and limited information on studying and learning Hungarian in Hungary.

Hungarian National Tourist Office
PO Box 4336
London SW18 4XE
Telephone: 0891 171200

ICELAND

Embassy of Iceland
1 Eaton Terrace
London SW1W 8EY
Telephone: 0171-730 5131
The embassy is not encouraging people to look for work in Iceland at present as the economy is in recession and the level of unemployment is high. However, it can provide information on studying and learning Icelandic in Iceland.

IRELAND

Irish Embassy
17 Grosvenor Place
London SW1X 7HR
Telephone: 0171-235 2171
The embassy provides basic information on living in Ireland and contact addresses for job-seekers.

The Irish Higher Education Authority
21 Fitzwilliam Square
Dublin 2
Telephone: 00 353 1 612748
The Irish Higher Education Authority provides information on studying in higher education in Ireland and the fees for courses.

Irish Tourist Board
150 New Bond Street
London W1Y 0AQ
Telephone: 0171-493 3201

ISRAEL

Embassy of Israel
2 Palace Green
London W8 4QB
Telephone: 0171-957 9500
The following universities in Israel have contact people in London offices who can give information regarding studying at their university: Hebrew University, Tel Aviv University, Haifa University, Ben-Gurion University, Technion, Weizman Institute of Science, Bar-Ilan University. The embassy may provide information about voluntary work in Israel, limited information on working in Israel (a work permit is needed), addresses of Hebrew teaching courses and schools and information on the politics, history, society, culture and education system in Israel.

Friends of the Hebrew University of Jerusalem
3 St John's Wood Road
London NW8 8RB
Telephone: 0171-286 1176
The School for Overseas Students at the Hebrew University offers a five-month course from February to June for students between school and university. Summer courses are run in a wide variety of subjects including Arabic, Hebrew and Yiddish. One-year courses include a programme of Jewish, Israel and Middle East studies and

a postgraduate course (in English) at the Faculty of Social Sciences and Humanities.

ITALY

Italian Embassy
14 Three Kings Yard
London W1Y 2EH
Telephone: 0171-312 2200
The embassy provides general information on the history, culture and geography of Italy.

The Italian Institute
39 Belgrave Square
London SW1X 8NX
Telephone: 0171-235 1461
The Institute provides general information on Italy plus information on working, studying and attending Italian language classes in Italy. For information write in with your request enclosing an SAE.

Italian State Tourist Office
1 Princes Street
London W1R 8AY
Telephone: 0171-408 1254

LIECHTENSTEIN
Covered by Swiss Embassy (see page 253).

LITHUANIA

Embassy of Lithuania
17 Essex Villas
London W8 7BP
Telephone: 0171-938 2481
The embassy provides general assistance on working in Lithuania, particularly as a teacher of English.

LUXEMBOURG

Luxembourg Embassy
27 Wilton Crescent
London SW1X 8SD
Telephone: 0171-235 6961

A list of student organisations and educational courses is available. Send an SAE.

Luxembourg Tourist Office
122 Regent Street
London W1R 5FE
Telephone: 0171-434 2800

THE NETHERLANDS

Exis (Centre for Youth Activities)
Postbus 15344
1001 MH Amsterdam
Prof. Tulpstraat 2
1018 HA Amsterdam
The Netherlands
Telephone: 00 31 20 626 2664
Exis KLIX arranges au pair positions in The Netherlands.

Netherlands Board of Tourism
PO Box 523
London SW1E 6NG
Telephone: 0891 200277

Royal Netherlands Embassy
38 Hyde Park Gate
London SW7 5DP
Telephone: 0171-584 5040
The embassy provides information on learning Dutch and working in The Netherlands and a range of booklets. It also produces *A Guide for Young Visitors.*

NEW ZEALAND

New Zealand High Commission
New Zealand House
80 Haymarket
London SW1Y 4TQ
Telephone: 0171-930 8422
The High Commission provides general advice regarding studying in New Zealand and holds newspapers and business and telephone directories to which job-seekers can

refer. The New Zealand Trade Development Board (telephone: 0171-973 0380) provides an information pack for UK/foreign students wishing to study in New Zealand. The New Zealand Immigration Service (telephone: 0171-973 0366) provides work visa information. The High Commission does not provide lists of companies or situations vacant in New Zealand.

NORWAY

Norwegian Embassy
Counsellor for Press and Culture
25 Belgrave Square
London SW1X 8QD
Telephone: 0171-235 7151
The embassy does not help people find employment but will give advice to those wanting to go to Norway to find their own job. It produces a booklet called *Foreign Students in Norway* and can give information on universities and learning Norwegian in Norway.

POLAND

Embassy of the Polish Republic
47 Portland Place
London W1N 3AG
Telephone: 0171-580 4324
The embassy provides information on short-term work in Poland (including English language teaching) and provides contact addresses in London. It also provides general information about the Polish government's graduate or postgraduate scholarships, addresses of universities, entry requirements and length of courses, application procedures. Addresses and requirements of universities in Poland that organise language courses and information about fees and booking can also be provided. Finally, the embassy holds information about cultural events taking place in London and Poland.

Polish Cultural Institute
(a branch of the Polish Embassy)
34 Portland Place
London W1N 4HQ
Telephone: 0171-636 6032/3/4
The Cultural Institute provides information for candidates interested in teaching English in Poland. Its work also includes promoting artistic and scientific contacts with Polish organisations and institutions, running a library of Polish books and reading room for Polish papers (English versions available), organising lectures and meetings, and operating Polish Government Grants exchange scheme with the British Council.

Young people may be interested in the following services offered by the Cultural Institute:

- Polish language courses for beginners and advanced learners (Tuesday evenings)
- Information on the Polish education system
- Information on the higher education opportunities and university courses available for foreigners
- Information on Polish Government Postgraduate Scholarships in the fields of sciences, humanities and arts
- Information on scholarships for a four-week stay in Poland to study the Polish language at universities participating in the Polonicum scheme including The Warsaw University, The Jagiellonian University in Cracow, The Marie-Curie Sklodowska University in Lublin and The Catholic University in Lublin
- Full information on all governmental and private Polish language schools in Poland
- Information on bursaries for short visits to Poland (up to three weeks) for individuals visiting Poland for academic and professional purposes.

Polish Tourist Board
82 Mortimer Street
London W1N 7DE
Telephone: 0171-637 4971

PORTUGAL

Canning House
The Hispanic and Luso Brazilian Council
2 Belgrave Square
London SW1X 8PJ
Telephone: 0171-235 2303
Information leaflets costing £3 each are available on study courses, opportunities and employment in Spain, Portugal and Latin America. Canning House also runs language courses in the UK. Contact Head of Education Department.

Portuguese Embassy
11 Belgrave Square
London SW1X 8PP
Telephone: 0171-235 5331
The embassy provides some general information on higher education and working in Portugal.

Portuguese National Tourist Office
22–25a Sackville Street
London W1X 1DE
Telephone: 0171-494 1441

RUSSIA

Intourist Moscow Ltd
219 Marsh Wall
Isle of Dogs
London E14 9PD
Telephone: 0171-538 8600
Intourist organises tours and independent travel to the countries of the former Soviet Union.

Russian Embassy
13–15 Kensington Palace Gardens
London W8 4QX
Telephone: 0171-229 3628
The Russian embassy can advise people wanting to study or learn Russian in Russia.

SLOVAKIA

Republic of Slovakia Embassy
25 Kensington Palace Gardens
London W8 4QY
Telephone: 0171-243 0803

SPAIN

Canning House
The Hispanic and Luso Brazilian Council
2 Belgrave Square
London SW1X 8PJ
Telephone: 0171-235 2303
Information leaflets costing £3 each are available on study courses, opportunities and employment in Spain, Portugal and Latin America. Canning House also runs language courses in the UK. Contact Head of Education Department.

Instituto Cervantes
102 Eaton Square
London SW1W 9AN
Telephone: 0171-235 1485
The Instituto Cervantes provides information on universities in Spain and publications are available for consultation at the Institute. It also has publications, a database and prospectuses on Spanish language courses at universities and private language schools in Spain. Students can obtain information by visiting the Institute or writing enclosing an SAE. The Institute also runs Spanish classes.

Spanish Embassy
20 Peel Street
London W8 7PD
Telephone: 0171-221 0098
The education office encourages the learning of Spanish while the labour office provides general information on working and living in Spain, job centres, terms and conditions of employment, employment and unemployment statistics, social security benefits, etc. It does not, however, deal with vacancies.

Spanish Tourist Office
57 St James's Street
London SW1A 1LD
Telephone: 0171-499 0901
The tourist office can provide names and addresses of Spanish hotel chains for those looking for jobs in the hotel and catering industry.

SWEDEN

Embassy of Sweden
Cultural Section
11 Montagu Place
London W1H 2AL
Telephone: 0171-724 2101
The embassy provides information on study and summer language courses in Sweden and on entry regulations. There are currently no official programmes for youth exchange or short-term jobs.

SWITZERLAND

Swiss Embassy
16–18 Montagu Place
London W1H 2BQ
Telephone: 0171-723 0701
The embassy provides lists of universities, art colleges, music academies, hotel management and tourist schools in Switzerland as well as information on graduate courses and the Swiss government's postgraduate scholarship programme. It produces lists of schools in Switzerland

offering French, German and Italian (the three official languages) language courses to foreign students and holds general information on Switzerland. There are strict regulations for entering Switzerland. Work permits are required and are not easy to obtain. Contact the embassy for information on work permits.

Swiss Hotel Association
Department of Employment
Monbijoustrasse 130
PO Box 2657
3001 Bern
Switzerland
Telephone: 00 41 31 46 1881
The Association will provide information on employment in hotels.

Swiss National Tourist Office
Swiss Centre
Swiss Court
London W1V 8EE
Telephone: 0171-734 1921
The Swiss National Tourist Office can advise people who want to work in Switzerland.

Tourist Office Malcantone
Attention: Mr Alfonso Passera, Director
6987 Caslano
Switzerland
Telephone: 00 41 91 71 2986
Contact Tourist Office Malcantone for information on tourist office employment.

United States of America

American Chamber of Commerce
75 Brook Street
London W1Y 2EB
Telephone: 0171-493 0381

The Chamber of Commerce has produced a book of American firms and subsidiaries in the UK.

American Embassy
24 Grosvenor Square
London W1A 1AE
Telephone: 0171-499 9000
The embassy provides advice via a phone line to those wanting to enter the USA. It does not help people find employment in the US and refers job-seekers to UK national newspapers, trade journals and recruitment agencies in the UK seeking staff for US companies. For visa information telephone: 0891 200290.

American Institute for Foreign Study
37 Queen's Gate
London SW7 5HR
Telephone: 0171-581 7300
The Institute provides information on a USA study programme for young people between 15 and 18 and a half. Young people can stay with an American family and attend high school for a year.

Fulbright Commission
Educational Advisory Service
Fulbright House
62 Doughty Street
London WC1N 2LS
Telephone: 0171-404 6994 (10.30am – 4pm Monday to Friday)
The Fulbright Commission provides information on exchange programmes and courses in the USA. It produces a range of information sheets including *Study abroad programmes for secondary school students*, *Exchange programmes with the USA*, *Two year colleges in the US*, *GAP year study in the US*. It holds 800 prospectuses and American college guides and information on work exchanges. The Commission can also give advice to those wanting to study for an entire degree course in the US and the scholarships available.

Index